MW00617210

Preston Fidler beautifully integrates the twin missionary tasks of language learning and gospel communication. I highly commend *1000 Cups of Tea*.

David Garrison, author, *A Wind in the House of Islam* and *Church Planting Movements*

This is the book that I have waited through 50 years of cross-cultural missionary service for someone to write. Language fluency is at the very foundation of missionary service. Clear and understandable communication of the gospel is the very heart of missionary service. Preston Fidler has effectively built that bridge between acquiring language fluency and communicating the gospel so that hearers understand, believe, and live the good news of Jesus Christ.

Sam James, author, *Servant on the Edge of History* and *The Making of a Servant*

In *1000 Cups of Tea* Preston Fidler comes alongside those of us who may be discouraged in language learning or intimidated by the call to share the gospel cross-culturally and illuminates a path forward. This accessible, practical guide is the fruit of decades of experience learning to speak the gospel fluently. His sincere love for people and his passion for the hope of the gospel shines on every page.

Tina Boesch, author, *Given: The Forgotten Meaning and Practice of Blessing*

1000 Cups of Tea provides an eloquent and passionate description of how effective and fulfilling ministry can be when it is built on relationships made possible by cultural understanding and fluency in the language of the local people.

Carol Orwig, SIL International

1000 Cups of Tea meets a critical need that I experienced numerous times during 30 years of serving as a cross-cultural missionary. I was a language learner three times with different languages and learning systems. Later I informally coached dozens of language learners and eventually I assessed and made recommendations to language programs in numerous countries. This book gets it right! It is not enough to know how to buy vegetables or say "hello." Learning language is about sharing good news and that should be integral from the beginning. Insightful and encouraging! This book should be read repeatedly by everyone who is learning a language for gospel purposes.

Don Dent, Director, Kim School of Global Missions, Gateway Seminary, SBC; author, *The Ongoing Role of Apostles in Missions: The Forgotten Foundation*

1000 Cups of Tea is an excellent account of a Christian cross-cultural worker that truly does the long-term work of language and culture learning so that Jesus would be known and glorified among the nations. Through reading Preston Fidler's relatable prose, heartfelt exhortations, and thought-provoking discussion questions, the reader is able to envision the humility, sacrifice, servanthood, and joy that comes with a lifetime of language learning and gospel ministry.

Natalie Mullen, Ph.D., Institute for Cross-Cultural Training, Wheaton College

Learning a second language as an adult is one of the most profound ways to express genuine care for a person from another culture. *1000 Cups of Tea* provides compelling inspiration for committing oneself to this arduous task for the sake of the eternal.

David Broersma, Associate Professor of TESOL and Linguistics, Lee University

I wish I had read *1000 Cups of Tea* 25 years ago! Preston Fidler's book gives struggling language learners a clear path forward, challenging us to take steps every day to speak God's word to others. We don't have to wait until we reach a certain language level or "test out" of full-time study. Whether you are a new learner or a veteran of overseas life, this book will help you see how language learning can be a joy filled, Scripture saturated process.

Sarah Alexander, Lead Writer, *Along the Silk Road: Stories, Reflections and Photography*

Preston Fidler's *1000 Cups of Tea* is simply a book on imitating Christ. As Preston's and Jenn's pastor, I can attest first-hand that they live "gospel fluency" by communicating and reflecting Christlikeness not just in words, but in deed and truth! *1000 Cups of Tea* will intensify your desire not just to be fluent in one's new language to share the gospel, but to be fluent in living the gospel, fluent in hearing and obeying the promptings of the Holy Spirit and fluent in the very language of God and His Kingdom! *1000 Cups of Tea* will propel you to an even higher call of your faith in Christ, your faithfulness to the work and your willingness to imitate Christ in every area of your life!

Mike Fritscher, Pastor, Cottonwood Church

1000 Cups of Tea is down on the ground, in the trenches, uber-practical wisdom, borne from experience and toil. You may be a new language learner, laboring to get to the place of being able to share the gospel for the first time. You may be a seasoned vet trying to stay sharp so that the gospel will be even more clear to your friends. You may be a discouraged language learner, thinking about throwing in the towel. I urge all of you to read what Preston Fidler shares.

Dean Polk, Church Planting Team Leader, Central Asia

1000 CUPS OF TEA

FIELD GUIDE

BY PRESTON FIDLER

First Edition

Copyright © 2021 by Preston Fidler

ISBN 978-1-7356042-2-0

Unless otherwise indicated, all Scripture quotations are taken from: The Christian Standard Bible. Copyright © 2017 by Holman Bible Publishers. Used by permission.

Illustrations and sketches by Jenn
Copyright © 2021 All rights reserved

Front cover, logo, design, and artwork by Eric Schmidt
Copyright © 2021 All rights reserved

Table of Contents

Introduction   i

1 | Gospel Fluency   1

2 | Eyes Wide Open   7

3 | The Gospel for My Lost Neighbor   17

4 | Simple Familiar Gospel Story   25

5 | Gospel Radius   36

6 | Responsive Listening   49

7 | LQ   62

8 | Deep and Wide   75

9 | Language 180   101

10 | 1000 Cups of Tea   114

11 | God Speaks My Language   128

12 | Pilgrims   143

Conclusion   167

Endnotes   174

Introduction

People often ask me what it takes to become fluent in a new language. I tell them it takes a thousand cups of tea.

1000 Cups of Tea: Field Guide helps language learners get to the heart of gospel fluency across cultures. Use it as a companion to *1000 Cups of Tea: Gospel Fluency Across Cultures,* or read it by itself as both a book and field guide to work through these core concepts and outcomes:

- Understand the basics of gospel fluency across cultures.
- Align your perspective with God's perspective on gospel fluency.
- Evangelize your lost neighbors as you learn their language.
- Comprehend and tell simple familiar gospel stories in your new language.
- Engage your neighbors through the limitless radius of the gospel in all life encounters.
- Learn to listen and respond as an integral part of the fluency needed to reach neighbors with the gospel.
- Know what it means to intelligently learn a language.
- Invest in life-long language learning.
- Practice *Language 180* for fruitful ongoing learning and in-language ministry.
- Converse the gospel in your new language.
- Share your testimony; pray for your neighbors.
- Identify as a Kingdom pilgrim, with an unwavering assurance in your destination and an insatiable desire to invite others to join you from the "nations of every language" (Zechariah 8:23).

PEOPLE OFTEN ASK ME WHAT IT TAKES TO BECOME Fluent in a LANGUAGE. I TELL THEM IT TAKES 1000 Cups of Tea

How to use this Field Guide

We have to reframe our understanding of the boundlessness of gospel fluency. Ultimately, our investment is not in the hours and tasks. It's in the relationships.

Take a moment to look over the core concepts and outcomes on the previous page. These summarize the content and goals for each chapter you read in *1000 Cups of Tea: Field Guide*. You may be just starting out as a language learner and much about "gospel fluency across cultures" is new for you. You may be an experienced field worker who just needs to be reminded and encouraged to re-engage in language and ministry. Whether you are a beginner or a seasoned veteran, I hope that as you read and work through *1000 Cups of Tea: Field Guide* you will be able to more fully understand and apply these concepts and practices to your life.

Each chapter begins with a goal, ends with a summary, and then guides you to "reflect and respond" and to consider your "next faithful step" before moving on. In other words, goals and summaries bookend each chapter followed by questions and thoughts that invite you to reflect and respond to the driving themes and lessons found throughout the Field Guide. For example, the goal of Chapter One *Gospel Fluency* is "to understand the basics of gospel fluency across cultures" and the summary describes the chapter as "a testimony of gospel fluency across cultures" followed by a *Reflect and Respond* section that begins by asking you to, "Describe a recent experience when you personally shared the gospel with someone."

As you read, reflect upon, and respond to the questions and thoughts following each chapter, consider your next faithful step by answering the question, "What is one way you resolve to put what you have learned into practice?" For example, upon reading Chapter One, a possible *Next Faithful Step* response may be, "I will prayerfully consider my motivation for learning a new language." Summarize your thoughts in *My Next Steps to Gospel Fluency* found at the end of the Conclusion of the Field Guide.

Additional articles, lessons, and resources can be found at www.language180.com or by scanning this QR code using the camera app on your phone.

language 180

1

Gospel Fluency

Goal: Understand the basics of gospel fluency across cultures.

We proclaim him. Colossians 1:28

Toward the end of our first year in our new field, Jenn and I were trying to learn a new language, set up work, and at the same time were expecting our third child. We were busy, struggling language learners. One morning, I read through Matthew 8:5-13, the story of the centurion who asked Jesus to heal his servant. I could understand it but expressing my thoughts in my new language was a challenge. I read it in English, prayed, and wrote out my thoughts. I did the same in my new language, only slower, much slower. It was pretty ugly, but it was a start. And I believe it was the first step toward sharing the gospel with my neighbor over tea later that day.

I had scribbled down a few notes in my new language that gave me some traction to say something meaningful about the story and stay in the conversation with my neighbor; that the centurion was a man of military authority, that his servant was dying, that he (the centurion) believed Jesus could save his servant.

When the centurion came to Jesus to ask for help, Jesus offered to go and heal his servant. But, the centurion, because of his unworthiness, declined to have Jesus come to his home. He went on to say that he knew the meaning of authority. He himself had a boss, and he obeyed his boss. He had men under him to whom he gave orders, and they obeyed his orders. "I am not worthy to have you come under my roof. But just say the word, and my servant will be healed" (v. 8).

As a man who understood military authority, this centurion acknowledged Jesus' supreme and total authority. Just as he believed Jesus could heal his servant right then and there, he believed Jesus was Lord over everything! Jesus was amazed at the centurion's faith, and because of his faith he healed his servant and invited him into the Kingdom of God.

With these scriptures and well-rehearsed notes in my hand, head, and heart, I met my neighbor for tea. Conversations never go quite as planned in situations like this, so I have learned to be flexible and try to stay in step with what I sense God is doing. There is a certain balance between preparation, delivery, and stewarding a sympathetic awareness of the flow of conversation as it reroutes in directions we may not expect, yet can anticipate, because that's how God works. God opens doors we may not even know are there.

We can learn to proclaim the gospel to our neighbors in our new language from God's word, through our witness, in our conversations, and as we pray. We are never just pursuing language fluency. We are pursuing what I am beginning to understand as *gospel fluency*[1].

I had been praying for my neighbor, asking the Lord for favor in our time together, that he would see the truth of the gospel through our conversation. My language was still so weak, and I felt that I was in way over my head. I knew so little about his world and his culture, but I prayerfully trusted God's guidance in the conversation. I wondered if asking some questions related to his life and the topic would be a good place to start. I tried to be engaging and specific, listen to the Lord, and do my best to listen to my neighbor.

In simple words, I shared this gospel story from Matthew 8. I asked about my neighbor's view of authority – in his own life, in his family, and in his community. We talked about God and unseen powers, what we fear, and what we trust. I invited him to consider the truth we learned from the Bible: that Jesus has authority over everything – sickness, evil, sin, and even death. We talked about God's kingdom, his plan of salvation, and what it means to place our faith in Jesus.

I probed a little deeper, knowing my neighbor had served in the military. To my dismay, his face went ashen. He became quiet. I didn't know what was going on, but we had obviously touched a nerve. He whispered of abuse he had experienced, mentioning something about his commanding officer, an evil person, forcing him to commit atrocities he wanted to forget, but couldn't. He sighed deeply. The conversation drew to a close. I had no idea what was going on in his heart.

We often face communication challenges and barriers such as these when we communicate the gospel in another language. Does our message make sense? Do our weak language skills create barriers to the gospel? I hadn't been in the country very long. I was just learning to share the gospel in my new language, and those first steps are never easy.

When we feel the tension between the conviction to evangelize our lost neighbors, and the inability to do so adequately in their language – at least in our own estimation – we need to remember that in situations such as these we can easily lose sight of the underlying victory and purpose of our cross-cultural witness. We risk losing a fresh and vibrant word from the Lord when our efforts to express a daily witness succumb to the pressure of performance and the fear and frustration of potential failure.

Cross-cultural life and ministry can be brutally humbling, requiring a certain endurance that can only be sustained by strength in our Lord, not in ourselves. In addition to the normal stress of cross-cultural life, we carry an extra burden, the duty to learn to speak well in another language, so we can proclaim Christ clearly. How can we be sure to effectively communicate the gospel in our new language? Do we depend on Christ's strength in and through us, in this process? What may normally shut us down in weakness may just become the pivotal strength of our testimony, bearing vibrant witness to the gospel of Jesus Christ.

> What may normally shut us down in weakness may just become the pivotal strength of our testimony.

The next morning at 3 a.m., my phone rang. It was my neighbor. He had just had a dream about his military experience. His commander was once again ordering him to do something terrible. He was angry and afraid. Suddenly, a higher commander appeared beside him, assuming complete command and bringing peace and complete authority to the situation. My neighbor woke up and he immediately knew this new commander was Jesus, the one with supreme authority. I rejoiced in hearing this news and had the awesome privilege to lead my neighbor to faith in Christ that day!

God surprised me. He reminded me that the path toward gospel fluency is a humble journey of many faithful steps. I

4

often look back at that experience when I face communication challenges. I had been faithful with what little I had. God had multiplied it. What I'm talking about here is not merely language learning. Rather, it is a fresh look at the joyful fruit of proclaiming the gospel in another language to our lost neighbors.

The vision is simple: we as cross-cultural Christian workers need tools, but more than anything else we need a godly reason to learn the language. I endeavor to provide both. *1000 Cups of Tea* reminds us of the joy we can experience in sharing the gospel with our precious neighbors as we learn our new languages; that language learning is something we don't *have* to do *before* we share the gospel, rather something we *get* to do *while* we share the gospel.

> We get to learn the language
> while we share the gospel with
> our precious neighbors!

Chapter Summary

-   A testimony of gospel fluency across cultures.

Reflect and Respond

1. Describe a recent experience when you personally shared the gospel with someone.

    _____

    _____

2. Imagine reading through a simple, familiar gospel passage in your new language. What is the language?

What is the passage? Where are you? (For example, "I am having tea with a neighbor in my kitchen...")

_____

_____

_____

3. *Language learning is something we don't <u>have</u> to do <u>before</u> we share the gospel, rather something we <u>get</u> to do <u>while</u> we share the gospel.* Reflect on this statement. What stands out to you?

_____

_____

_____

4. Take a moment to pray for your neighbors and to pray for opportunities to share the gospel them.

My Next Faithful Step

Describe one way you resolve to put what you have learned from Chapter 1 *Gospel Fluency* into practice. (For example: "I will prayerfully consider my motivation for learning a new language.")

_____

_____

2

Eyes Wide Open

Goal: Align your perspective with God's perspective on gospel fluency.

"Look, I tell you, lift up your eyes, and see that the fields are white for harvest." John 4:35 ESV

I sympathize with the disciples who returned from buying bread and were surprised to see Jesus talking with a Samaritan woman (John 4:27-35). They couldn't figure out what Jesus was doing, so they just told him to eat something. I'm sure that's what I would have said, too.

Then Jesus shifted their perspective. They were thinking about bread, but he was thinking about souls. Like the disciples, my thoughts are usually on the next daily task, and that may even include learning a new word in my target language. My "food" is so often just about me and my small world. Jesus' food was to do God's will. He invited his disciples to lift up their eyes and see not grain, but souls white for harvest. Picture Jesus' disciples literally lifting up their eyes to see a whole Samaritan village – yes, non-Jews, foreigners – coming down the street toward them, eager to hear more about the living water Jesus offered the woman.

So often as language learners we find our attention reduced to just getting the next word or phrase. Jesus calls us to a new perspective as we learn language and reach out to our lost neighbors with the gospel. Jesus calls us to lift up our eyes (v. 35).

Gospel fluency often represents a shift in our perspective on language learning in our cross-cultural Christian ministry. Language learning is no longer just about the words and paragraphs, rather about relationships, and sharing the gospel with those around us who need to hear it. When duty becomes a delight, burdens become a springboard. We find joy in hearing and speaking the gospel to ourselves in the language we are learning, as our daily manna, and in sharing the gospel with our neighbors, as our daily ministry.

When duty becomes a delight, burdens become a springboard.

We endure the challenges of language learning setbacks when we don't experience progress. But with every gospel story we tell, and every passage we explain, we find joy in inviting people to follow Christ. One language learner recently told me that her entire first four-year term was being overshadowed by a proficiency level she was told to reach. I responded with this word of encouragement:

> Please do not let language proficiency goals distract or distress you from the overall goal – the ability to proclaim and teach the gospel in your new language.

Everything we do in language learning is to become fluent in our interpersonal communication of the gospel. Our first goal, therefore, is to get to the point where we can begin to do this. This means more than working through a single prepared presentation. It means conversing on multiple simple gospel passages. We must learn to tell them clearly, explain them simply, and dialogue about them informally. We must be able to talk about how the gospel impacts our lives in simple words of testimony. *This* is gospel fluency, and rest assured this gospel fluency goal certainly correlates with proficiency levels we are trying to reach.

God shifts our perspective in language and ministry to align with his. And we're in good company. The pages of Scripture and Christian history generously testify of prophets and apostles whom God awakened to a fresh and dynamic awareness of his message of redemption, to see their call from his perspective, not their own.

In Exodus 3-4, God revealed himself to Moses from a burning bush, commissioning him to lead the nation of Israel out of their bondage in Egypt. God promised his presence to guide Moses as he spoke with Pharaoh. Moses was afraid, had no confidence in his ability to speak, and doubted God (Exodus 4:10). Contrast this with God's glory radiating from Moses' face as he descended Mount Sinai (Exodus 34:29-35).

God's presence was with Moses in both circumstances. But as he came down from the mountain the lingering effects of God's presence brilliantly reflected the glory which he had experienced (Exodus 33:18-34:8). Do we bask in the glory of the gospel? As glorious as Moses' transformation seems, let's remind ourselves that unlike Moses, whose face radiated a fading glory of the old covenant, we host the never-fading presence of God through the power of the gospel (2 Corinthians 3:13-18).

Do we enter into gospel conversations with doubt and fear in our personal weakness, or with faith and courage, confident in the power of God, and in the message of the gospel? The presence of Christ in our lives compels us to proclaim the gospel. We are being transformed into his likeness, from glory to glory. We host his presence in our lives at all times, even as we proclaim him to our lost neighbors.

A saint shines on men when God has shone on him. (C.H. Spurgeon)

Jeremiah received a dramatic call as a prophet to the nations (Jeremiah 1:5). He, like Moses, also protested, "Oh no, Lord GOD! Look, I don't know how to speak since I am only a youth" (1:6). Though he doubted his ability to communicate God's message, God had appointed Jeremiah over nations and kingdoms (1:10).

God led Jeremiah to preach a message of judgment that was very difficult to preach, and equally hard to hear (19:6-9). The people's reaction was predictably harsh (20:1-2). Just released from the stocks, bruised and bloodied from the beating, Jeremiah bitterly complained, "You deceived me, LORD, and I was deceived… the word of the Lord has become my constant disgrace and derision" (20:7-8).

It's what Jeremiah says next that brings great comfort to me. Though he suffered greatly in his calling to preach a hard message devoid of any apparent hope, his hope and trust remained in God alone.

> I say, "I won't mention him or speak any longer in his name." But his message becomes a fire burning in my heart, shut up in my bones. I become tired of holding it in, and I cannot prevail (Jeremiah 20:9).

Memorize this verse! Unlike Jeremiah, we have a message of great hope and gladness. Ours is not a message of destruction. God calls us to proclaim his salvation for all peoples. The sad and perplexing mystery why anyone would reject this good news is overcome by the glorious mystery of the gospel – why God would ever love us enough to save us from our sins! This is the gospel we proclaim. We are compelled (Acts 4:20, 1 Corinthians 9:16). Like Jeremiah describes, the word of God is a fire in our bones. We are weary of holding it in.

The message of the gospel compels us to learn the language of those to whom we are called. Our confidence is in God and in the message of the gospel he has given us to live out and to proclaim. God ignites our hearts with the power of the gospel. The good news of God's salvation consumes our lives.

> God, I pray thee, light the idle sticks of my life and may I burn for thee. Consume my life, my God, for it is thine. (Jim Elliot)

Consider Peter. The restoration and reinstatement Peter received from Jesus on the beach in the wake of his devasting denial of our Lord (John 21:15-17) ushered him into an incredible ministry of spiritual fruitfulness, authority, wisdom, faith, miracles, love, and power (Acts 2:14-5:42).

Yet in the wake of this dynamic ministry, Peter experienced an unexpected shift in his spiritual understanding that caused him to pause and really consider the breadth of God's purposes for his life and for the world around him, introducing him to a totally new dimension of his calling. While in prayer, God called Peter through a vision to preach the gospel to those he was still unable to view in his mind and heart as recipients of God's grace – to non-Jews, outsiders from other cultures. This was, again, life changing for Peter (Acts 10:10-16).

While Peter was wondering about the meaning of the vision, some men who had traveled several days in search of him arrived at the gate of the home where he was staying, having been sent by a man named Cornelius, a God-fearing Gentile. An angel of the Lord had visited Cornelius and had instructed him to send for Peter (Acts 10:1-8). This was all a part of God's remarkable plan.

Something indeed had shifted in Peter's mind and spirit as a result of this vision from the Lord. Peter had been called to love God and feed his sheep, but Peter was still unable (unwilling?) to consider Gentiles as God's sheep, until he had this vision on the roof.

Peter returned with the men to meet with Cornelius. And after hearing Cornelius' testimony, Peter testified how God had changed his heart, opened his mind, and shown him his heart for the nations. This was an incredible breakthrough for Peter, a new and fresh understanding of God's purposes and calling for his life – to love God and feed his sheep, from every fold and every nation (Acts 10:34-35).

Cornelius and those in his household believed in the Lord Jesus Christ and were baptized (10:48). Through all this, the realization that only God could have done this was the most significant for Peter. Only God could have orchestrated this whole series of events culminating in the salvation of Cornelius and his household. Only God could have changed the heart of a stubborn Jew who then became his unexpected witness to the Gentiles. God had done it in Peter's heart, on the beach. And he did it again, while Peter was praying on a roof, and then again in a Gentile's home.

... and this word is the gospel that was proclaimed to you. (1 Peter 1:25)

Hudson Taylor is most remembered for the immensity of his Great Commission vision, faith, and supreme contribution to the task of taking the gospel into inland China, a task he personally described as "worth living for and worth dying for."[2]

His life and ministry in China provide us with such an amazing expression of what it means to live out the Great Commission in the middle of immense adversity. There he buried four of his eight children along with his first wife.[3]

In 1900, during the height of the Boxer Rebellion, the China Inland Mission, which Taylor led, lost more members than any other group: 58 adults and 21 children were killed.[4]

In the wake of this tragedy, Taylor held tightly to the promises of God when all else seemed hopeless. "I cannot read, I cannot pray, I can scarcely even think – but I can trust."[5]

One might think this would have been a good time for Hudson Taylor and his CIM colleagues to give up and go home. They didn't. Instead, experiences like this brought Taylor to a deeper, more radical, and complete dependence on God than he had ever known possible. "Complete surrender" became his secret to sustaining a fruitful and long-lasting ministry in the middle of raging challenges and adversity – what he personally described as the "exchanged life" (Galatians 2:20).

In other words, it wasn't the outer circumstances or accomplishments that concerned him, rather his inner life in Christ. John Piper said of Taylor's life, "This new yieldedness was so powerful and so sweet – so supernatural – that it rose up like an indictment against all vain striving."[6]

> The living God still lives, and the living Word is a living Word, and we may depend on it.
> (Hudson Taylor)

What stands out to me is not what Hudson Taylor *did*, but who he *was* in Christ. It was his humble, enduring, singular devotion to Christ characterized by overwhelming, enduring peace, and "soul rest" that sustained his life-long vision to reach every unevangelized province in China with the gospel. Taylor's own son and daughter-in-law offer this amazing portrait of the normal everyday life of this servant of God as they traveled with him. Don't let the formal nature of this account distract you from noticing the deeply personal and powerful influence Hudson Taylor's life in Christ must have had not only on him, but also upon all those around him.

> It was not easy for Mr. Taylor, in his changeful life, to make time for prayer and Bible study, but he knew that it was vital. Well do the writers remember traveling with him month after month in northern China, by cart and wheelbarrow, with the poorest of inns at night. Often with only one large room for coolies and travelers alike, they would screen off a corner for their father and another for themselves, with curtains of some sort; and then, after sleep at last had brought a measure of quiet, they would hear a match struck and see the flicker of candlelight which told that Mr. Taylor, however weary, was poring over the little Bible in two volumes [presumably, English and Chinese] always at hand. From two to four A.M. was the time he usually gave to prayer; the time when he could be most sure of being undisturbed to wait upon God. That flicker of candlelight has meant more to them than all they have read or heard on secret prayer; it meant reality, not preaching but practice.[7]

It is God who calls us to this perspective and into this practice, this inner-life expression of complete surrender, yieldedness, faith, and fruitfulness – where striving ceases, Christ becomes all in our lives, his word comes alive in our minds and hearts, and then overflows to those around us, even as we communicate the gospel in our new languages and cultures.

If you are ever drinking at the Fountain, with what will your life be running over? - Jesus, Jesus, Jesus! (Hudson Taylor)

When we honor the call of God to go to another culture, and to learn another language, we need to remember that when God called Moses, Jeremiah, Peter, Hudson Taylor, and so many others, he transformed their lives in the process. God revolutionizes our hearts and beckons us to *lift up our eyes* just as Jesus called Peter and the other disciples to do at the well (John 4:35). He shows us things we would never have otherwise seen. Unlike never before, we see those from other cultures who speak other languages. We become mindful of the message of the gospel we must proclaim. As God is at work in our hearts, even now, God is pursuing the hearts of those we may not even know yet, whose languages we may not even speak yet.

Chapter Summary

- Jesus called the disciples in John 4:35 to "lift up their eyes."
- When God calls us, as he called Moses, Jeremiah, Peter, Hudson Taylor, and countless others, he aligns our perspectives with his.

Reflect and Respond

1. Read each verse below and describe in a phrase or short sentence the shift in each of their perspectives (For example: *Moses went from being "filled with fear and doubt" to "abiding in God's presence and reflecting his glory."*)

   Moses (Ex 33:18) _____

   Jeremiah (Jeremiah 20:9) _____

Peter (Acts 10:34-5) _____

Taylor (Galatians 2:20) _____

2. How might you respond to what Jesus said to the disciples in John 4:35? Share one way that God has opened your eyes to see more of what he is doing in your life, through your life, and in the lives of those around you today.

    _____

    _____

3. Consider this question: *Do we enter into gospel conversations with doubt and fear in our personal weakness, or with faith and courage, confident in the power of God, and in the message of the gospel?* Ask this question of yourself and respond.

    _____

    _____

My Next Faithful Step

Describe one way you resolve to put what you have learned from Chapter 2 *Eyes Wide Open* into practice. (For example: "I will reflect on how my perspective needs to re-align for the cross-cultural task to which God has called me.")

_____

_____

_____

3

The Gospel for My Lost Neighbor

Goal: Evangelize your lost neighbors
as you learn their language.

And he asked Jesus, "And who is
my neighbor?" Luke 10:29

It is no accident that in Luke 10 as we read Jesus' response to the question, he tells a story of a Samaritan foreigner reaching out to a Jew. Jesus is helping us understand what it means to proclaim the gospel to our neighbors as we cross ethnic and language boundaries. This is a prelude to the Great Commission. We must seriously consider that as we are called to obey the Great Commission and proclaim the gospel to all peoples we are called to personally bring the gospel to our lost neighbors in such a way that they can understand and receive the gospel. We choose to learn the language of our neighbors so that we can communicate the gospel to them. It's just that simple.

Jesus meant to redefine what many of us think it means to love our neighbor. The Samaritan, Levite, and priest all passed the same road and saw the same man stripped, beaten, and left half-dead. But only one reached out to him as a neighbor and responded to his needs – a foreigner. In fact, we know from the story that this Samaritan went to great lengths to care for this man.

> Jesus meant to redefine what many of us think it means to love our neighbor.

What efforts do we expend to reach out to our lost neighbors? Do they know the good news? Will we be the ones to tell them? Do we even know their language? I often ask myself these questions:

- When was the last time I shared my faith with my lost neighbors?

- When I ask myself that question, am I convicted? Filled with compassion?

- Do I have a regular practice of proclaiming the gospel to my neighbors?

- What am I doing in my life to be fluent in the gospel for my neighbors every day?

- How much time do I spend in God's word in my new language every day?

- How does this affect and reflect on my daily witness to those around me?

18

I introduced this with the question: When was the last time I shared my faith with a lost person? But, as I reflect on recent conversations that I've had with learners in tough places, maybe there is a prior question: Do I delight in sharing the gospel?[8] Because if I do, chances are I will also delight in learning the language of my lost neighbors who need to hear the gospel.

Do I delight in sharing the gospel?

What makes a successful language learner? Aptitude plays a part. But attitude plays a bigger part. Are we not thankful that we have the opportunities and resources to be able to learn our neighbor's language? Do we not deeply desire to reach a level of fluency so that we can clearly communicate the gospel to them?

I caution us against an entitlement attitude that expects and therefore only reaches minimum standards. This is a tragic perspective. Our minimum standard should be our baseline for really taking off in our learning and ministry. We get to do this! By God's grace we get to learn to share our faith in another language and reach out to our lost neighbors!

We get to do this!

If we regularly practice sharing our faith, chances are we will continue to do so as we practice learning the language. This affection, this practice, will drive us – not just to learn the language, but to proclaim the gospel to our lost neighbors in their language. And we will be thankful for every class we attend and every word we learn and use that puts us on this path toward fluency. I truly believe this grateful attitude – this *thankfulness* – is the best litmus test for determining our long-term language learning capacity and success. Our purpose is to tell the good news, and that purpose is what compels us to learn the language so we *can* tell it.

Just tell me the gospel again and again. (Richard)

This was my colleague Richard's daily motto and has become mine. Richard and I would meet with a couple of local brothers to read through Scripture and pray together each week in the local language. One of the things I learned from each of these brothers was how much we each need to hear the gospel. It was our ambition to speak the gospel into each other's lives when we met. It was such a personally enriching and deeply encouraging time in the Lord together.

Richard knew several languages, and he was more fluent in some than others. He would return from teaching in one where it "flowed like water" and then get back into the language we used together for our guys' time, which often didn't flow as well. Yet I never recall a moment when that distracted us from drinking deeply from God's word together.

We would take a book of the Bible and work through it together. We would remind each other of the gospel. So many times I recall Richard saying something like, "Would you look at that?" and we would down-shift and talk through the text, considering how God was calling us to respond. Are we not continually astounded by the beauty of the gospel, and God's marvelous, wonderful grace in our lives?

Keep it simple, accessible. When we are in first gear, we get to see everything. (Richard)

Lydia loved sharing her faith with her neighbors, and she did a great job learning the language so she could do this. She reached a point where she was able to have many life-changing heart-to-heart conversations. One evening I got a call from Lydia describing a recent fruitful conversation with her good friend M.

Lydia compared it to an experience so wonderful, it just takes your breath away. She first asked, "Have you ever skied down a slope at the end of the day after a fresh snowfall?" And then said, "Well, multiply that by 1000, and that's how I felt when I knew what I was saying was reaching M's heart."

Nothing remotely compares to this joy. This is the joy of the shepherd who found the lost sheep! This is the joy in the presence of God's angels when one sinner repents!

Dave is starting his third language. It's not easy, but he's motivated to learn. Like Lydia, Dave has a passion to share his faith. Dave has a fire to preach the gospel. And that fuels his language learning. Recently, he wrote,

> During our last couple years in [a previous location], I remember thinking at one point 'I can't remember when I've last gone a day without sharing some Biblical truth with someone.' It's been much more difficult to do that here but finally, in the past couple of weeks, I feel like I'm at a point language-wise to do that. I still don't have natural opportunities to share every day that I'm out but probably more than half. Hopefully, as I continue to grow in language and find better ways to ask better questions that will naturally lead to spiritual conversations, I will have more opportunities to share and will be able to share better.

Recently, I had the privilege of meeting with a team doing ministry in a large city. Josh, the team leader, gave a word of personal encouragement, "I used to share the gospel every day back home. Since arriving here, I felt that I'm just learning the language. But today…today is different. Today I experienced something I haven't experienced in a long time, like a memory from the distant past, another life."

Josh went on to describe the joy of communicating the gospel in his new language to a neighbor. And it was more than just a few sentences. That was important for him to emphasize, and I'm glad he did.

Josh said what made the difference was that he just had to entrust both his language abilities and his language limitations to the Lord. He talked about how he practiced telling a simple Bible story, how he learned to relate his testimony to it, and how he worked and worked on communicating them fluently. By the time he told them, even though there were some mistakes, it was understandable. And the point is, he did it. And he has also found someone to help him work on making it better.

I was inspired to help others follow Josh's example. I recently shared with a group of team leaders doing ministry in other languages, who were also supervising language learners, "I challenge you, and I want you to challenge your team, to dig deep into the word of God, in your new language, every day, as much as possible." Here's what I exhorted them to consider:

> Read one simple passage. Get one simple take-away. Work on one simple testimony. Get help from people who are one or several steps ahead of you. Have at least a part of your daily personal Bible study and prayer in your new language. Then with a Bible in your hand, and the word of God in your head and in your heart, rise from your knees to bring the gospel to your lost neighbor.

The results? More people began to experience the insatiable joy of telling the gospel story in the language of their calling. They realized that this was within their reach, that it didn't have to take a long time to get there. We just accelerated this process with some good language learning practices. Easy, right? Far from it. It was hard work. But it was a labor of great joy because of the results. Richard summed it up well:

Learn to communicate the Good News at every step of language learning through gospel-centered relationships and gospel language content. You need to learn gospel content, but you also have to *use* that content in order for it to stick. It takes deliberate practice. Build fluency as you learn ever more challenging gospel language pieces and share that gospel language with others who give you helpful feedback. Seek to improve as you learn from them how to do better. Rinse and repeat that cycle. Again, and again.

Chapter Summary

- Jesus' parable of the Good Samaritan helps us to better understand what it means to love our neighbors.
- As we delight in sharing the gospel with our lost neighbors the gospel permeates our lives and our conversations.

Reflect and Respond

1. Think of five of your neighbors who do not yet know Christ – perhaps they are from your hometown, workplace, college, or new city. Resolve to share the gospel with them. Write down their names, and beside each name a specific prayer of intercession.

1. _____   _____

2. _____   _____

3. _____   _____

4. _____   _____

5. _____   _____

2. Consider the question: *Do I delight in sharing the gospel? Because if I do, chances are I will also delight in learning the language of my lost neighbors who need to hear the gospel.* Reflect on this statement. Describe what it means to delight in sharing the gospel with your lost neighbors, so that it permeates your life and conversations.

_____

_____

_____

My Next Faithful Step

Describe one way you resolve to put what you have learned from Chapter 3 *The Gospel for my Lost Neighbor* into practice.

_____

_____

_____

4

Simple Familiar Gospel Story

Goal: Comprehend and tell simple familiar gospel stories in your new language.

But Jesus said, "Let the little children come to me." Matthew 19:14 ESV

Not long ago we were meeting with the family of a young lady my wife led to the Lord – the grandmother, her son, the son's daughters, their children, and the aunt of one of the daughters. We read through this simple story of Jesus blessing the little children from Matthew 19:13-15 and I invited the family to respond. The young lady who had just come to Christ earlier that day, told her family that she was like one of those children. Having faced many obstacles, she thanked Jenn for leading her to Jesus. And she thanked Jesus for inviting her to come to him. We experienced the joy of hearing each person in that room share one by one from their hearts a new and fresh understanding of what it means to come to Jesus.

The gospel is not complicated. The New Testament is full of simple familiar gospel stories, just like this one, that speak of coming to Jesus in simple, childlike faith. We identify with these stories. We came to Christ in much the same way. And we get to tell these simple stories, including our own, when we share the gospel with people.

In Mark 10:46-52, a great crowd was following Jesus as he left Jericho, and a blind beggar named Bartimaeus shouted out to him, "Jesus, Son of David, have mercy on me!" Those around him rebuked him, telling him to be silent. But he cried out all the more, "Have mercy on me, Son of David!" Jesus called him. And those around him said, "Have courage! Get up; he is calling for you." And throwing off his cloak, he sprang up and came to Jesus.

> "Have courage! Get up; he is calling for you." Mark 10:49

In Mark 2:1-12, Jesus was teaching in a crowded house. Four men brought a paralytic to him, but they could not enter through the door because of the crowd. As they were not able to get their friend in need to Jesus, they removed the roof from above where Jesus was teaching. When they had broken through, they lowered the mat on which the paralytic was lying.

In Mark 5:25-34, a great crowd was following Jesus when a woman who had suffered from bleeding for twelve years came up behind him in the crowd and touched his garment, for she said, "If I just touch his clothes, I'll be made well."

In each of these stories, people came to Jesus to receive healing and salvation. In each situation, they came while facing considerable physical and cultural opposition. They did not politely ask to see Jesus. They resisted opposition and found a way to him. They ran, they climbed, they pushed, they dug, they begged. This is how they came to Jesus – in childlike faith. If we ever wonder what Jesus meant by that phrase, here it is:

unrefined, uninhibited, risky, unconventional, hope-filled, desire-filled, God-ordained, out-of-the-box faith. In each of these lives, Jesus explicitly and audibly recognized their faith. He forgave them and healed them because of their faith, and because he could. Isn't this how we come to Jesus? He is the answer to all of our needs. He is the giver of salvation. This is our testimony, too.

I love the immediate declarative thanks and praise, words of testimony that we hear from so many who came and received healing and salvation from Jesus. "When the woman saw that she was discovered, she came trembling and fell down before him. In the presence of all the people, she declared the reason she had touched him and how she was instantly healed" (Luke 8:47).

Of the ten lepers who were healed, one returned to Jesus. "He fell facedown at his feet, thanking him. And he was a Samaritan" (Luke 17:16).

As we teach the gospel from these simple familiar stories, we can invite our neighbors with full confidence in the power of God's word, exhorting them to come to Jesus with this same kind of faith. People they know, communities they live in, even their families may try to dissuade them from coming to Christ. Beliefs, shame, fears, and doubts may all contribute to a lack of faith. But Jesus is calling them, as he calls us all, to follow him.

In Matthew 14:22-33, Jesus' disciples were in a boat on the sea. Jesus came toward them walking on the water. The disciples were terrified. Jesus told them to have courage, and to not be afraid. Peter said, "Lord if it is you, command me to come to you on the water."

Jesus said, "Come." Climbing out of the boat, Peter started walking on the water and came toward Jesus. But when he saw the strength of the wind, he was afraid and began to sink.

"Lord, save me!" Peter cried. Jesus caught Peter's hand as he was sinking. Rescuing him from drowning, Jesus then rebuked Peter for his doubt and lack of faith. Doubt and fear are strong deterrents to faith. Peter was in way over his head, literally! We sometimes experience this. I have seen eyes glaze over as I share the gospel. Fears rise. Doubts multiply. It's crazy, isn't it? When we invite our neighbors to come to Jesus in faith, it's a life-changing proposition. Flesh resists the truth.

We need to tell this story. We need to tell every gospel story: the unexpected salvation of Zacchaeus, the sobering response of the rich young ruler, the joy of the lost son who was found by his father, and the polarizing anger of his older brother. People need to know that the journey to Jesus is a strong call, that faith is real, and though sin and flesh are crouching at the door, redemption is at hand.

The beauty of these stories is that they simply speak the gospel. The fundamental theme in each of these passages is that people did come, and that they came to saving faith in Jesus, by the grace of God. Each of these stories provides vibrant illustrations of faith, of people who came to Jesus in faith, and therefore came to faith in Jesus. We can point to these living examples as we invite and persuade our neighbors to do the same.

> The beauty of these stories is that they simply speak the gospel.

We as language learners need to understand what it really means to tell *simple familiar gospel stories* as we learn our new language. As we learn to tell these stories, we don't learn them in a vacuum. We are simultaneously learning the basic *texts* or *discourses* of life going on around us, the back-and-forth of stories that define who we are before our neighbors and help us understand them. In other words, as we learn to talk with people, and as we learn to share the gospel, we are learning the basics of how to discourse in our new language.

Discourse is conversation, discussion, and dialogue; it's the meaningful topics we think about and therefore learn to talk about. Simple, direct, and concrete, the ebb and flow of our basic expression or discourse ability in our new language slowly begins to usher us into the fabric of our neighbors' lives.

There is a strong relationship between the ability to sustain a basic conversation in our new language on familiar topics, and the ability to understand and tell simple familiar gospel stories. We should never separate these two skills. Though one may be an *interpersonal communication skill* (dialogue), and the other a *presentational speech skill* (story), we cannot and should not develop one without the other. We are called to present the gospel. However, more importantly, we are called to converse the gospel. People will respond. We need to be able to understand and attend to their responses in meaningful ways.

We may be asking the question, "At what level can we tell a simple gospel story?" Rather than levels or timeframes, let's consider discourse ability. What functional abilities do we need in the language – rote phrases? sentences? paragraphs? – to be able to tell a simple, familiar story? Understanding our functional ability in the language can help get us on the right track as we consider true progress.

Any meaningful language interchange we have with those around us is discourse. We begin with simple words and phrases, and progress to sentences, then paragraphs, and finally entire discourses. As this happens, our ability to dialogue improves. When we describe a picture, listen and respond to a story, explain events from our lives, or discuss truths from the Bible, that is all discourse. Discourse is the ability to speak, listen, and dialogue.

Speaking and hearing a new language begins with the most predictable and simple phrases and sentences. As we progress, we are able to speak, understand, and respond in broader and deeper ways to a growing number of familiar and unfamiliar topics. With growing complexity, our paragraphs become a rich discourse of stories, descriptions, and discussions on all topics of life.

As we look down the road of greater *gospel fluency*, we picture the ability to confidently and extemporaneously describe, narrate, explain, and discuss many simple and familiar redemptive topics that we have worked through. We are better able to see and grasp how we can begin to effectively teach the Bible to our friends and neighbors in their language.

As we imagine the ability to dialogue about these topics, we begin to see how our responses are no longer simple sentences. Rather they are robust paragraphs that allow us to engage in meaningful discussions with our neighbors. We can envision the outcomes of this teaching, the fruit of this ministry God has given us.

These represent the content and expression, the "nuts and bolts," of *discourse fluency*. These are what we need to be thinking about when we consider fluency in the language and, therefore, fluency in ministry. *Discourse fluency* is the ability to describe, narrate, explain, and persuade in meaningful topics of interest, with minimal or no preparation, through speaking, dialogue, and responsive listening. *Gospel fluency* is the practice of discourse fluency using redemptive content.

For years I've used a helpful little chart to help direct learners to correlate ministry outcomes with language levels using the ACTFL scale.[9] We will not look at formal definitions; I want to focus on the discourse outcomes. As we look through the following descriptions, let's consider the functional ministry we could do at each of these language levels, and the discourse fluency we may need for each of these tasks.

Discourse Fluency and Ministry Outcomes

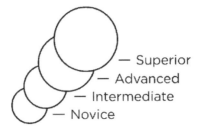

— Superior
— Advanced
— Intermediate
— Novice

Novice

- Use phrases about God
- Distribute tracts
- Initiate relationships
- Share memorized words of blessing

Intermediate

- Pray for people
- Ask questions about faith
- Share testimony
- Tell simple Bible stories
- Weave in some basic truths

Advanced

- Read the Bible for meaning
- Ask deeper questions
- Pray more fluently
- Teach a simple Bible study
- Lead and participate in basic discipleship

Superior

- Lead deeper discipleship
- Develop and instruct leadership training
- Participate in Biblical counseling
- Teach

One of the things I like about this chart is that when we look at it, we immediately can see some things that we can do or should be able to do soon. This is what I mean by functional ministry descriptions. We see these descriptions as things we can do, based on our language ability.

As a language coach and disciple-maker in her new language, Amy has thoughtfully expanded the language tasks related to this chart simply by asking the question, "What can

I do in church?" I love this question! *This* is the question we should all be asking ourselves as we pursue *gospel fluency*. We no longer learn a language simply to reach a level. Rather, we actively practice *doing* something eternally meaningful in the language with those around us and are therefore inspired to keep learning. Because the more we learn, the more we can do.

As a cross-cultural evangelist, Meg developed the *Good News Skeleton with Hand Motions* to help us learn to share the gospel in our new languages starting with these sixteen-sentences.

> In the beginning there was God.
> God created the first people.
> They had a perfect relationship with God.
> But people disobeyed God, they sinned.
> People were separated from God.
> Sin is a barrier – to be with God.
> How can we remove sin?
> Only God can remove sin.
> God became a person and lived among us.
> That person was Jesus.
> On the cross, Jesus took our sins and became the sacrifice.
> Jesus died, was buried, but on the 3rd day he rose from the dead.
> Because of Jesus, a relationship with God is possible.
> I believed in Jesus, and my sins were forgiven.
> According to the Bible, God's Spirit filled me.
> Do you want your sins forgiven through Jesus?

The *Good News Skeleton* is like a simple story we learn to say in in our words, which we can expand upon with explanations, descriptions, gospel passages, and testimonies as our language grows. It is best learned by watching the video and practicing right along with Meg. You can find Meg's *Good News Skeleton* along with Amy's "What can I do in church?" at www.language180.com or scan the QR code found at the introduction and conclusion of the book.

There is an interesting correlation between language level and how much one is able to actually do in the language at that level. At the *Novice* level, there is very little we can do in the language. Notice, though, that as we progress into the *Intermediate* level, and into each successive level, how much more we can do in the language. Notice how much more ministry we can engage in, how many more ministry outcomes we can expect.

Considering this, where on this chart would we actually reach the ability to understand and tell a simple familiar gospel story? Remember, this is not about reciting a memorized story, nor is it a story told in isolation of conversational ability on a range of familiar topics. It may be helpful to view this ability – the practice of understanding and telling a simple, familiar gospel story – as the fulcrum of our language learning, the tipping point with the capacity to infuse the rest of our language learning journey with joy. In a very real sense, the simple, familiar gospel story is that for which we are aiming, *and* from which we spring-board. It's the effectual turning point in our language learning that gives us the drive to keep going. If we get to a place where we can understand and tell simple familiar gospel stories, we muster the inspiration to keep learning. When we reach basic narrative comprehension and presentation abilities, this puts us squarely on the path toward sustained discourse fluency – that is, *gospel fluency*, giving us both the language skills and the spiritual acuity to proclaim the gospel in our new language.

Chapter Summary

- Understanding and telling simple familiar gospel stories from the Bible.
- A thoughtful approach to discourse fluency through considering ministry outcomes.

Reflect and Respond

1. Envision yourself retelling one of the narratives (stories) mentioned in this chapter in your new language. Which story is it? Write 1-2 sentences about the story.

   _____

   _____

   _____

2. Describe one thing you can work on that will improve your ability to share the gospel from simple familiar Bible stories?

   _____

   _____

   _____

3. Do you have someone who can help you with this, perhaps a language partner, national partner, team-mate, or neighbor? Take a moment to pray for that person.

My Next Faithful Step

Describe one way you resolve to put what you have learned from Chapter 4 *Simple Familiar Gospel Story* into practice.

_____

_____

_____

For more resources about learning how to understand and tell simple familiar gospel stories go to www.language180.com or scan the QR code found at the introduction and conclusion of the book.

5

Gospel Radius

Goal: Engage your neighbors through the limitless radius of the gospel in all life encounters.

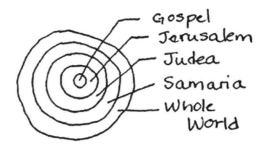

for the promise is for you and for your children, and for all who are far off, as many as the Lord our God will call. Acts 2:39

Mehmet heard the gospel for the first time in our local house church in the town where we lived. I met with Mehmet several times after that and sensed his struggle with sin. He had a rough marriage but was stubborn and did not surrender his life to Christ. After we moved, I continued to pray for Mehmet.

Several months later I received a phone call from a friend who lived in our city of 18 million people, several hours from Mehmet's hometown. James shared with me that as he had been walking through a busy part of the city the day before, he had felt impressed to share the gospel with a certain guy sitting on a bench, and that guy was Mehmet. Mehmet told James that he had heard the gospel in his hometown from me. Once it all became clear to Mehmet that James knew me, it suddenly hit him, "How did God find me in this huge city?"

That evening the three of us met for tea. "This shouldn't be happening," I thought to myself. Only God could love Mehmet so much to pull this off. As we read and talked through the parables of the Lost Sheep (Luke 15:1-7) and the Lost Son (Luke 15:11-32), we marveled together at how much God loves us, that he loves Mehmet, and *that* is the reason he pursued him all the way to the city. Mehmet had come to be with his girlfriend. Instead, in the middle of millions of people, God chased him down. That's just the way God works.

The radius of the gospel is limitless. It reaches people in all life situations and speaks to the human condition at every level. The buoyancy of the gospel sustains every conversation so that as we proclaim the gospel, we live it; and as we live it, we cannot help but proclaim it. When we open our eyes, we see the Holy Spirit at work in people's lives as God woos them to himself in the context of our daily interaction.

We bear the gospel in simple powerful witness through the stuff of shared life, in homes, over tea, and at work. The discourse of the gospel should encompass the entire radius of our discourse ability in our new language, using everything we know in the language, covering all topics. As we begin to view our lives through the lens of the gospel, all conversations become those precious opportunities we are given to communicate the gospel to our neighbors.

> *We have to reframe our understanding of the boundlessness of gospel fluency. Ultimately, our investment is not in the hours and tasks. It's in the relationships.*

Our lives truly intersect with the world around us, the world God called us to, in powerful and true ways, in ways that demonstrate spiritual integrity when we hone-in on the gospel. Are we orienting the core of our lives to the gospel? Until we view the gospel as the center of everything in our lives, then our entire global and cosmic orientation remains faulty, worldly.

After his resurrection Jesus instructed his disciples to stay in Jerusalem. He told them the Father's master plan for the kingdom, that by the power of the Holy Spirit they would be his witnesses in Jerusalem, Judea, Samaria, and to the ends of the earth (Acts 1:8). We stake our lives on the truth of this verse. This is our commission. This is the ever-widening radius of the gospel, both geographic and ethnic in nature.

Acts 1:8

Gospel
Jerusalem
Judea
Samaria
Whole World

The expanding radius of the gospel is also personal in nature. As the gospel changes our lives, and as we are called to proclaim the gospel to our lost neighbors, and then to their neighbors, in and through just about every walk of life conceivable, we get a micro-view of this ever-expanding radius of the gospel. As the gospel is spreading to all peoples, it spreads from neighbor to neighbor, and from community to community. And we are personally responsible to be a part of that process.

Our neighbors are found in all domains of our lives. They live in the apartment next door to us. They live across the street. They may be parents, children, or relatives of those who live next door, or across the street. They are those we work with and buy from. They may run the fruit stall or drive a taxi. And they are all within the radius of our daily lives and need to hear the gospel. In every situation, every relationship, and through all conversations, we can communicate to the gospel through our daily encounters with our precious neighbors.

Gospel Radius

The Gospel
The Gospel in my life
The Gospel for my neighbor
The Gospel for my neighbor's neighbor

These concentric circles of identity and relationship begin with the gospel as core to all that has eternal meaning in the world. It is core to our identity and to our relationship with God. The gospel radiates from our proclamation of the word of God and is able to reach and redeem our neighbors through every life circumstance and situation we share with them. The gospel is not just a concentric ripple. It is a vector that has the power to reach in and transform every part of our world and the world around us. Is it possible for us to be *that* aware of the ever-permeating effect of the gospel as we carry the very presence of God into all areas of the lost world God has called us to reach?

We are called to love our neighbors, which means we tell them the gospel because we love them. Where I live, that almost always means over tea, through shared life events, and usually involves family members and neighbors. I've heard this referred to as the enlistive blessing of God (Acts 2:39). I call it "the gospel for my neighbor's neighbor."

Andrew and Simon were brothers, and Philip and Nathaniel were friends, and they were all neighbors from the same hometown, Bethsaida. Jesus invited Andrew to come to his home. Andrew then invited Simon to meet Jesus, whom Jesus then named Peter. Jesus then called Philip to follow him. Then Philip invited Nathaniel to come and meet Jesus (John 1:35-51). Each invitation led to an invitation, which probably led to another invitation.

"Come and see", Philip answered.
John 1:46

I recently had tea with Metin and his contractor, Ziya, who is also one of the elders of our house church. Ziya remodels houses. Metin has several houses in the area and entrusts Ziya with all the work he does to them. Metin has cancer and probably doesn't have long to live. Ziya and I prayed for Metin as we drank tea. We prayed for healing. We prayed he would receive salvation through faith in Christ, the ultimate healing for his soul. I was so thankful that Ziya sees his business as a place of ministry to guys like Metin.

One of Ziya's employees is from an unreached minority ethnic group. Not long ago Melih had a serious accident at work requiring extensive surgeries on his hand. As he recovered at home, Ziya invited me to visit Melih and his mother. We shared the gospel with Melih and he translated into his mother tongue for his mom to understand. Ziya lives out the gospel as he works with Melih and the other guys. He is not just their boss. He in many ways is like their older brother. They listen, watch, and take it all in. Ziya is sowing seeds of the gospel with Metin, Melih, their families, and so many other neighbors at work and through his business.

One of the things I really appreciate about Ziya is that he is quite aware of the gospel at work in the lives of his neighbors, customers, and employees in everyday ways. He is learning to present the gospel and that's one of the reasons he invites me to come along. As I disciple Ziya, we pray for his neighbors, and for opportunities to preach the gospel clearly and boldly. For Ziya, this means living and sharing the gospel at work and at home. He can't see it any other way. That encourages me to be more aware of the activity of the word of God in the lives of my neighbors in everyday situations.

We see this in Jesus' ministry. He dined with tax collectors and Pharisees. He broke bread with his disciples. He met people at their places of work. He talked with farmers and told them about the kingdom of God using farming analogies. He talked to rich people and challenged them to follow God by selling their possessions. He rebuked other rich people for their greed in comparison with the generosity of a poor widow. He blessed children, raised dead sons, taught people in their homes, and taught them in his home. He attended weddings, had late night discussions, and asked for water on a long hot day's journey.

How can we present and proclaim the gospel well in all circumstances? How can we view the centrality of the word of God in all seemingly tangential topics and discussions? How can we learn about life and culture around us so that we understand how the gospel is reaching our neighbors through the stuff of their lives?

I recently received a phone call from Ziya. He was on his way to our city to visit Metin in the hospital. Metin was close to death. His wife called for Ziya to come. They had no one closer they could turn to during this time of fear and grief. Ziya then called me. I was honored to join these precious friends at Metin's bedside as once again Ziya shared the hope and comfort of salvation in Jesus Christ with Metin and his family. As we talked and prayed over tea before leaving the hospital, I was reminded of how only God could orchestrate all this because he loves us so much.

Spheres of Influence

We have a finite number of people that we can invest in. Are we willing to lay down our relationships in our home community in order to create space for new connections,

relationships, and identity, within our new language and
culture community? (Josiah Daniels, co-worker)

As I write this, I am looking at a still-life picture on our wall that my wife, Jenn, painted in our neighborhood women's art class. I call it her "Van Gogh." It's splotchy, but it's beautiful. Lots of great color, almost 3D in effect. It's a painting of a grape vine with branches full of ripe grapes, like you would find anywhere here in Anatolia. It is surrounded by the words of Jesus from John 15:5.

Jenn and I pray for these art-class ladies. Many of them are religious. Most are skeptical. It would seem they are impossible to reach for the gospel. But we pray for these ladies. We ask the Lord for divine curiosity to fill the art room, that these ladies would wonder just what this spiritual grape vine is all about.

Several of the ladies began to approach Jenn, asking her about her painting and why she was stenciling verses from our New Testament around the grape vine. Jenn explained that we, as followers of Jesus, are like branches, drawing nourishment from Jesus, our vine, to produce life-giving fruit. She shared the gospel from John 15.

The ladies were intrigued. They understood the beauty of this spiritual illustration about life and about God. They knew the cultivation of grapes like the backs of their hands, but they had never seen it in this light. As she finished her painting, Jenn continued the conversation day after day, sharing the gospel. Several of the ladies have asked for a copy of the New Testament. As for the painting, it's hanging on our wall, ready as a gift for a neighbor, for the next time she comes over to have tea with Jenn.

Our neighbors rarely evaluate Christianity by reading about it. They watch us. They talk with us. (Timur, national partner)

When we think of the radius of the gospel, we need to understand that it has an all-pervasive effect on every area of our lives and the lives of our neighbors. Do we believe this? Do we live with this kind of expectation? Do we learn and practice language with this understanding? This takes faith, boldness, and creativity.

As we consider sharing Christ with our lost neighbors, how can we grow in our understanding of gospel-relevant themes, so that our gospel-sharing is conceptually more connected with where they are?

We are not just trying to build bridges to the gospel. We need to understand and believe that they are already there. We simply need to discover them and find ways to cross them.

What would be natural bridges to the gospel for every topic that I engage in? And how would I get to the gospel from that topic? (Josiah Daniels, co-worker)

Jenn looks for all kinds of bridges to the gospel with our neighbors, whether through art, crafts, music, or simple life stories. Recently, she created a wordless tract illustrating the tragic yet beautiful life and death of a young child – a child who could easily have been one of our neighbors' neighbor. As we've shown this tract to different people, reactions have ranged from weeping to sharing a personal experience. Everyone identifies with it in some way. It's amazing how one simple story made up of a few illustrations and no words (except at the end) has opened the door to so many amazing gospel conversations.

Color (not visible here) first appears in the tract as a red heart and red cross on the "Jesus loves you so much" leaflet the little boy finds. As he reads it and believes, the little boy and everything around him become full color. All is radiant as Jesus receives the little boy's soul into in his arms, while the boy's body remains a black and white shadow in the box. The tract concludes with three gospel passages on the final page: John 3:16, Ephesians 2:8-9, and Romans 10:9-11, 13. (You can find the full-color version of this wordless tract at www.language180.com or scan the QR code found at the introduction and conclusion of the book.)

I had a friend in my city give me some great advice as I was learning the language. "Talk about anything and everything with people you are getting to know. If you show an interest in everything about their lives and talk about everything in your life, and don't hesitate to talk about God, it will become clear to you and your friends how God is at work in every aspect of your life, and theirs."

This advice helped me be purposeful and move forward in language, enriching my relationships with people more broadly and deeply. How did I go about doing this?

I began to observe what was going on around me more intently, carrying a notebook, taking notes, and writing down questions that came to mind as I noticed things. This would help me be more prepared at any time with things to talk about, and questions to ask, as I had conversations with people.

I began reading things about the culture: articles, short stories, magazines, and current events from newspapers, even cutting out and using pictures as conversation starters.

I began listening more to the radio and following TV and online programs in the language, starting with the basics – headlines, a few words here and there – enough to launch me into conversations about specific topics.

It's amazing how asking open-ended questions on so many topics seems to touch everyone's life in some way. I found that following my friend's advice not only improved my language ability but provided great invitations into peoples' lives and opportunities to see God work in their lives.

> You want to know where God is working? Share the gospel and you'll find out! (Mark, co-worker)

Our lives intersect with our neighbors in multiple overlapping spheres or segments: work, school, religion, family, community. People buy, sell, care, host, converse, argue, love, play, cry, and laugh together. Life happens in community. We are family and we have family. We are neighbors and we have neighbors.

The New Testament refers to some of these spheres as households (Acts 16:31-34). Where I live, we call them life circles. These are the *liminal* "coffeeshop" spaces where people find community – where life happens, but also where lives change. God takes us into these life spaces to be with people – our neighbors – and to engage them, in big ways and small ways. God invites us into his redemptive work in their lives through this dynamic of life-in-community, however great or incremental, obvious or hidden.

We should never diminish the amazing work that God is doing right now and right here in the lives of our neighbors, the people in our communities. We need to engage. We need to commune. We need to love deeply. We need to learn the language of the day-in and day-out life we share with our neighbors, as we communicate the gospel to them, every day.

Chapter Summary

- The radius of the gospel is limitless, from God using James to chase down Mehmet, to Ziya sharing his faith at work, to Jenn using a wordless gospel tract with neighbors.
- Acts 1:8 represents the expanding radius of the gospel on a global level, which can also be seen on a personal level as "the gospel for my neighbor's neighbor."

Reflect and Respond

1. What stood out to you from Mehmet's, Ziya's, or Jenn's stories?

   _____

   _____

   _____

2. Reflect on this statement: *I didn't get to share the gospel today because it didn't come up in our conversation; we were talking about other things that weren't relevant to the gospel.* Briefly explain how the gospel can be a relevant part of every conversation.

   _____

   _____

   _____

3. Consider future gospel opportunities with your neighbors. Describe your present anticipation, awareness, and responsiveness to those opportunities.

   _____

_____

_____

4. Consider how you invest in the lives of your lost neighbors. Take a moment to pray for opportunities to share the gospel with your lost neighbors through all conversations of life.

My Next Faithful Step

Describe one way you resolve to put what you have learned from Chapter 5 *Gospel Radius* into practice.

_____

_____

_____

6

Responsive Listening

Goal: Learn to listen and respond as an integral part of the fluency needed to reach neighbors with the gospel.

Your word is a lamp. Psalm 119:105

I watched and listened as Dinch shared his faith with Erol – Bible open, asking questions, inviting Erol to tell his story, finding points of connection, probing, and persuading Erol to a walk of faith in Jesus Christ. Dinch was an evangelist. He was an eager witness to his neighbors, tapping into their hunger for God.

On the ride home as we talked Dinch helped me connect the dots between the gospel message and Erol's situation. Dinch seemed to have a knack for knowing how to reach into people's lives. Something he said made me think long and hard. Dinch told me the main reason he asked so many questions and dug deep with Erol on certain issues was because he wanted to be sure that he was understanding Erol, and that Erol was understanding him.

That's right – my national partner Dinch, in talking with Erol in their heart language, needed to make sure Erol had understood him. I had to have him explain to me what he meant. Dinch wanted to ensure the message of the gospel was clear, not just from his perspective, but from Erol's as well. He wanted to make sure Erol understood what he was trying to communicate. For that reason, Dinch said, he did his best to patiently and wisely attend to Erol's responsiveness. How did Erol understand the gospel from Dinch's witness? Dinch's aim was to clarify the gospel, as much as possible, for Erol's understanding, not just for his own.

I came away from that experience contemplating my level of fluency in my new language. Dinch's convicting words set me back on my heels. Was I truly listening to my lost neighbors when I shared the gospel with them? Was I understanding their responses? Was I attending to their responses? Were they hearing the gospel, really?

> I find that even though I am starting to understand what people say, I often misunderstand what they mean. (Steve, first year learner)

We often think we are communicating more than we really are. The message of the gospel is communicated not only in the words we say. It is also, essentially, communicated in how we understand and respond to our hearers, as they hear the message, to be sure they understand the message. How can we better listen, understand, and attend to their responses to the gospel? How can we effectively understand and respond to our lost neighbors when they inquire about the gospel? This is the art and practice of *responsive listening*.

Responsive listening is more than just a surface understanding of what people say. We may think we understand people. But the truest test of comprehension is not in our passive understanding, rather in how honestly we verbally and non-verbally attend to what we hear, responding meaningfully and appropriately.

We must learn to listen and respond to how people receive the message of the gospel. Otherwise, we risk misunderstanding what people are hearing, and therefore miscommunicating the message of the gospel. To listen with understanding and to respond with godly wisdom are precious jewels in our language learning, cross-cultural evangelism, and disciple-making; arguably more challenging to master than speaking, and in some respects more valuable.

Listening: The Fountain Head of Gospel Fluency

Take care how you listen (Luke 8:18).

God's word is a lamp. Shining the light of the gospel into lostness calls for a deeper observation, a practice of spiritual discernment, a habit of listening and responding. We, in our own strength, ultimately cannot discern how a person receives the word of God. Only the Spirit of God illuminates.

What is hidden will be made known, what is in the dark will be illuminated. As I understand the integrity of the gospel (Luke 8:16-18, Mark 4:21-25) we carry this lamp initially for our deeper awareness, to see and hear what we need to perceive and understand, to reveal what has been concealed, and to boldly proclaim the gospel with the godly and sympathetic compassion of Christ.

> If anyone is thirsty, let him
> come to me and drink. John 7:37

God speaks to us from his word and by his Spirit. We need to listen. Jesus invites us to drink deeply. Jesus went on to say that he who believes "will have streams of living water flow from deep within him" (John 7:38). We hear and attend to the word of God as it reaches deep into our souls and are compelled to tell the message of the gospel to those around us. I've heard this described as living out of the overflow of the gospel in our lives. This image beautifully captures a faith-filled posture of *responsively listening* to God's word.

This posture compels us to attend to the message of the gospel. Our hearts and minds are quickened with sharper conviction, assurance, compassion, and authority. As we listen to God speak to *us* from his word and by his Spirit, we believe he is *also* ministering to our neighbors in ways that only he can do. God invites us to enter into this ministry through prayerful awareness and hope-filled anticipation.

And as we hear from God and trust that he is at work in the lives of our neighbors, we approach listening to our neighbors with a deeper awareness of God at work in their lives. We practice *responsive listening* right then and there, in those moments we engage them, hear from the Lord, and preach the gospel.

Our speaking skills are sharpened when we enter any conversation with a heart to understand the perspective of our hearers. This requires sympathetic awareness and understanding. As we learn to attend to those around us, we develop a cohesive posture of listening and speaking that helps us engage our neighbors with the gospel. Language is a paradox: Our best posture of speaking is one that attends well. Our best posture of listening is one with a compelling message.

We're not speaking to brick walls. (Sean, co-worker)

We have a couple at our house church who listens well. They listen. They pray. They ask questions. They offer encouragement and advice. They share Scripture. Then they

52

listen more. I love watching them in action. They provide amazing counsel for many believers. But they do the same when they share their faith with non-believers. And it's amazing to see the response. People open up. They share their burdens. They receive prayer gladly. They are comforted because someone has heard their story. And they respond to the gospel.

Listening is a huge investment. It is diving into the deep end of our conversations and discussions. It is total immersion – in our own language, tiring; in another language, absolutely exhausting. It takes total intentionality, requiring undivided attention, interpreting, question-asking, confirming, hypothesizing, re-confirming, adjusting, exploring, and more listening. The more we hear, the more we realize how little we know of the person, and of the situation. We keep digging, learning more.

Responsive listening skills help us develop insights into the lives of our neighbors and community. This is huge within any dialogical context, but especially as we practice evangelism and discipleship in our new language. We develop insights into the culture. We begin to understand communication nuances and apply them with greater fluency.

Responsive listening is a skill that only comes through hours and hours with people in tough communication situations during which we develop listening skills and are able to practice responding to people in ways that are culturally meaningful, biblically sound, and full of godly wisdom. As we are called to proclaim and teach the gospel, we are also called to listen well, and respond with understanding, as people hear and respond to the gospel.

How can we become fluent listeners in our new language? How can we learn to respond with anticipation and sympathetic understanding as the Holy Spirit works in people's lives? How can we effectively grapple with our bent toward conceptual rigidity and reach beyond our cultural myopia to truly understand our neighbors' view of the gospel in the reality of their own lives and situations? We must find a way forward toward greater fluency in our *responsive listening*, toward understanding and attending to their response to the gospel.

This kind of godly listening can be done in homes, over tea, in casual settings. People who may normally be somewhat closed to the gospel open up when they know someone cares enough to listen to them. This is often where people first really hear the gospel. Hearts soften and ears become attentive when people realize someone cares enough to listen and respond. One of the best ways to open up a flow of honesty and receptivity within our gospel conversations in our new language is to practice the art of listening, to make space to hear what people are really saying to us when we share Christ with them. I thought of Dinch and Erol. Listening really is the fountain head of gospel fluency.

Into the Unknown (Ethnography 101)

Go, ask questions, and listen. (Bill, co-worker)

As I passed his office on my way to work one day my accountant neighbor Hasan called me in to show me his broken fish tank. Sometime over the weekend while he was out and the office locked, his fish tank had mysteriously cracked from one side to the other and the water and fish had spilled out onto the new wood-paneled floor. Hasan reached down and showed me water damage that was already beginning to appear, shaking his head, concluding, "Someone vexed this office with the *evil eye*."[10]

The evil eye? Really? I confess, I was surprised and confused to hear this coming from a successful accountant. He couldn't have been more serious. "It is the look. Not what is seen, but what is looked at," as he proceeded to explain that obviously some of his neighbors must have been envious because of the new floor renovations. "Energy went from their eyes," pointing with his finger outward from the corner of his own eye, "and entered into this fish tank, causing it to crack precisely while I was gone," preventing him from being able to save the fish and keep the floor from being damaged.

Hasan had done everything he could to prevent this. He had strategically placed glass beads throughout the office, downplayed every compliment given about the fish tank and the new floor, and tried to make sure that no one – especially anyone jealous or angry –was able to release negative energy in his workplace.

What a complicated, fearful existence! It seemed Hasan's prime task in life was to protect against this ever-present evil. I began to notice just how pervasive this sort of practice was. People wore little pieces of glass resembling misshapen weird-colored eyes on their clothes, inscribed them onto objects, and pinned them on baby blankets. These eyes seemed to show up on every door, home, office, apartment, entry way, floor, sidewalk, store, decoration, piece of jewelry, and greeting card...they were everywhere! One thing was clear: my neighbors really wanted protection from evil.

Belief in this metaphysical malevolence, this evil, permeated everyday life. Accidents were attributed to the force of the evil eye: slips on the sidewalk, car accidents, sicknesses, broken fish tanks. Bad things happened to people because evil caused the bad things. Bad things were only avoided when protection against the evil causing the bad things actually worked.

This wretched fear-filled existence defined much of what my neighbors believed about the causes and effects of everything going on around them. I began to understand how people around me lived in fear, all the time. Their lives were consumed with trying to ward off the powerful effects of evil. But nothing could actually take away this fear. The fear itself seemed to fuel their vigilance to stay alive. Fear may have kept them alert to the ever-present threat of evil but robbed them of any peace they could ever hope to experience. And this was this world I had entered.

My encounter with Hasan reminded me that things are not always as they seem, especially for those of us entering new cultures and learning new languages. Whether it was the fear of the evil eye, or some other deep belief or worldview that formed who my neighbors were, what they did, and what they believed, I wanted to do whatever I could to reach an understanding of those "whys" in their lives. Working definitions (see endnote 10) certainly provided a good starting point for me to roll up my sleeves and begin to navigate the beliefs, traditions, and practices that enveloped the world in which I lived. But it was in conversations with my neighbors where I could actually ask the honest questions that helped me get to why. Did my understanding even vaguely represent the reality in which they lived? If so, how then could I reach into that world and begin to discover the *why* beneath so much of the *who, what, when, where,* and *how* I was seeing and hearing all around me? Not surprisingly, conversations with Hasan and other neighbors about these realities led to many more "broken fish tank" stories. All I had to do was ask. (To learn more about this, read *Getting to Why: Ethnography 102* found at www.language180.com or just scan the QR code found at the introduction and conclusion of the book.)

Countless conversations with neighbors helped me understand just a little bit more about their fear of this metaphysical evil power, and the all-consuming burden they carried to protect themselves against it. I began to see how these beliefs and practices were deeply woven into the fabric of their lives and culture. When asked, some acknowledged the power of the evil eye, while others dismissed it. But it seemed everyone respected or at least practiced the tradition of believing in the power of the evil eye and doing all they could to protect themselves against it. Perhaps this near-universal will to sustain the tradition and practice of warding off the evil eye represented a deep-set fear that even influenced those who brushed it off as mere superstition.

I have come to these insights cautiously and carry them gently as I continue to ask questions in an effort to peel back the layers of this evil, fearful world in which my neighbors live. I realize how much more I have yet to uncover. Asking my neighbors open-minded questions starting with the surface realities of daily experience that can lead to deeper questions of belief and worldview helps me to better understand them. As I've said, I just ask the questions. They tell the stories.

Asking questions and listening to responses are some of the best ways to begin to understand how our neighbors think and feel. This all starts with the power of wonder. As we suspend our preconceived ideas and assumptions to more fully participate in the amazing newness of life happening around us, do we wonder, "What is this?" or "What could this mean?" with a heart and mind to really learn from our neighbors? As we engage them in basic *who, what, when, where,* and *how* questions on all life topics, do we anticipate hearing everyday life stories within the texture of their responses? Can we begin to envision the deeper "whys" that may define what they believe and how they think?

As we attend to that which is going on around us and really listen to what our neighbors are saying – their interests, concerns, passions, and beliefs – we indeed find opportunities to dive a little deeper, beneath the surface of basic conversations, to understand more of the "whys" that encompass the contexts of their lives. Our ultimate desire is to understand and to then engage the spiritual needs of our lost neighbors, waiting expectantly upon God's grace as we introduce the gospel and invite them to respond.

Not long after my conversation with Hasan about the fish tank I was asked to help at a youth camp where kids from all over the country came and brought their friends to hear the gospel. On the last night of the camp, one young man who had recently put his faith in Christ shared his testimony before the group. He like so many others had grown up surrounded by what he could only describe as a resident evil power that had consumed his life and home with fear. He had literally lived with constant fear his whole life. And then he talked about the gospel in his life; how he came to faith in Christ, and how God had miraculously taken away his fear and replaced it with peace, concluding, "Could this even be possible?" The whole room grew quiet. Young people throughout the room began weeping. What this young man shared that night ministered to every heart. This is one of the most amazing realities Christians in my part of the world can share with their neighbors. God removes our fear and gives us peace.

First Responders

What they wanted even more [than the help that we were prepared to give] was for someone, anyone, even a stranger who was still trying to learn their language, to sit for a while, or just stand with them, and let them share their stories.[11]

As I write this my wife is visiting one of the first neighbors we befriended when we arrived to our city many years ago. Suna's and Mahmut's youngest son was the same age as one of our boys and they became friends. Doctors found a tumor in Han's brain and Han soon passed away. We were devastated. We grieved with our friends, prayed for them, and sadly watched them sink into a dark place which nearly disintegrated their family. Suna has always been open to Jenn's friendship, almost like a beacon in the night.

Every time they meet for tea, Jenn engages as a first responder. She just knows Suna cannot continue to cope without Jesus, so Jenn reaches out, prays, listens, and responds.

God has used this ministry to bring Suna to a place where hope begins. Jenn continues to meet with Suna, praying that God would fully bring Suna to a place of faith in Christ. "The person of the Holy Spirit gets us ready. He prepares us. He speaks to us even as we are conversing with our neighbors" (Jenn).

Engaging as a first responder means we are there, at the scene. And it also means we do what we can. We have no agenda. We come to listen. We empathize. We pray. We share words of comfort and the hope of the gospel. Often this is best expressed through the simple questions we ask – What happened? How do you feel? What's the most difficult part for you? – and, more importantly, how we choose to listen, just listen, as people respond.[12]

The Bible describes Jesus as knowing the thoughts of people's hearts (Luke 9:47). He had compassion, and he acted on it with godly understanding. One of our biggest opportunities is also one of our biggest challenges. When we respond to people in need, we will hear problems, issues, concerns, questions. When we minister truth with godly compassion, we see the life-changing effects of the gospel in people's lives. We must be attentive. We must be responsive listeners. This is hard work. This is the work of the gospel. "It's hard to believe in someone you don't know, but when you finally realize who God is, you won't want to follow anyone else" (Jenn).

People are hurting, desperate, and in pain. They need to know who God truly is. They need to recognize their need for his saving grace. They need to confess their sins. Behind the layers of sin and doubt, they long for the salvation, assurance, and hope that only the gospel provides. God calls us to listen and respond. But God doesn't leave us to ourselves.

When we attend to those responding to the gospel, when we seek to listen to them with understanding, we can trust that God is in the conversation. He knows our hearts, and he knows theirs. When we listen to others, we must first listen to God. He ministers to us through his word, by his Spirit. He gives us insight and understanding as we listen and respond to our lost and hurting neighbors. Our words – those we say, as well as those we hear – are powerful when they are an expression of our faith.

Zephir tripped and fell right in front of Yuri's house on her way back from the market. Yuri and his invalid wife Nelli host a small house church in a village near our home. Zephir and her husband had recently arrived with their grown son and had not met their new neighbors. Yuri saw what happened and quickly ran out, helped her up, gave her a glass of water, and invited her in to rest and talk with Nelli who was lying on the sofa.

Nelli asked a few questions and it didn't take long for Zephir to open up about the grief she felt because of her son's addictions, and the personal emptiness she felt in her heart. Yuri told me that from the moment he came to Zephir's aid, he sensed the guidance of the Holy Spirit in their conversation, providing insight into what God was doing, right then and there, in Zephir's heart.

We listen to what God is saying to us through prayer, through his word. This plays out in how well we listen to those we engage. As we engage them with the gospel, we need to be aware of how God is involved in the heart-level communication; how he is wooing people to himself, and how he is using us in that process. We need to be spiritually attentive.

Zephir prayed to receive Christ that evening. And Yuri continues to spend time with her wayward son, mostly just listening.

Chapter Summary

- Listening is the fountain head of gospel fluency.
- The gospel is our lamp as we learn to listen.

Reflect and Respond

1. Like Dinch, what is one way you can more actively listen to people when you share the gospel with them?

_____

_____

2. Consider Jenn and Suna, or perhaps Yuri, Nelli, and Zephir, and describe one way you can better listen and attend to your neighbors with the hope of the gospel when they share difficult life stories.

_____

_____

3. Take a moment to pray for spiritual insight and fluency to more meaningfully listen and respond to your neighbors in the language.

My Next Faithful Step

Describe one way you resolve to put what you have learned from Chapter 6 *Responsive Listening* into practice.

_____

_____

7

LQ

Goal: Know what it means to intelligently learn a language.

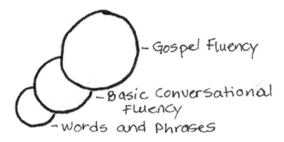

- Gospel Fluency
- Basic Conversational Fluency
- Words and Phrases

A language is learned rather than taught. (Tom Brewster)

I recently spoke with a group of newcomers entering new language settings. Each of them was a top-shelf candidate eager to learn. I asked them to articulate their goals, and they all responded by saying they wanted to learn as much as possible as quickly as possible. Several were parents with young children. At least one couple expected to manage a full-time business. I weighed their eagerness against the challenges. Young families? Starting a business? I wrote this note to them:

> The first few days, weeks, and months in the language are critical. Our incentive to learn is at an all-time high.

We are ready and willing to invest. We're willing to push through barriers, try new things, and work hard. We want results. We want to get the language. But we need to remember that equally important are those days which come long before day one in our new language. It is that day when we capture a vision to learn the language. It's that day when we can see ourselves gaining the knowledge and skills, devising the strategy, and tackling the project. It is those days when we can begin to articulate *why* we really want to learn the language. Then we can begin to seriously consider how we plan to learn it. This is intelligent learning. And it all starts well before we learn our first word.

We may have strong intentions to learn a language, but many of us struggle with what that really means, or what it's going to take. We need to begin to understand that we are never truly "taught" a new language, rather we personally and actively *learn* it. And the responsibility for learning a new language is ours and ours alone. That's a pretty simple truth, but it's so easy to forget, especially in the middle of daily language learning challenges. Personal responsibility is also the most important component to intelligent and faithful language learning. We need to understand what it means to really practice intelligent language learning in order to learn the language well, in order to reach *gospel fluency*.

> *The responsibility rests firmly on the learner's shoulders. A language is learned rather than taught.*[13]

"LQ" stands for Language Intelligence. Our personal LQ has far less to do with cognitive aptitude and far more to do with our power to discover and harness language resources we all have within us and around us. Intelligent language learning is made up of a combination of mindset, desire, skills, knowledge, strategy, and appropriate action. What does it take to be an intelligent language learner?

One of our greatest assets that compels us to be intelligent language learners is our calling to preach the gospel to all peoples. We have a strong desire to learn the language of our lost neighbors for the purpose of sharing the gospel with them.

But intelligent language learning is more than desire. Intelligent language learning includes the knowledge and strategy to wield that desire into action. And, perhaps most important, it essentially includes the investment of actually doing it. We can have all the best vision, motivation, knowledge, and strategy in the world, but without actually putting it into practice, we might as well go home.

I am disheartened when I hear language learners describe unsuccessful attempts to use programs, try techniques, go through lessons, or check off goals, when they fail to realize that it is not programs, lessons, techniques, goals, or strategies that yield success. Lessons and methods may serve to help us improve, only to the extent that we are truly invested in the language we are learning, and in the people who speak it. All vision, plans, and strategies, while significant as resources for intelligent language learning, still basically provide only the window dressing. Real change happens as we invest in learning new language, not through simply going to class or doing a program, but through the hard work of creative expression. We practice intelligent language learning not through completing a series of lessons, but through immersing ourselves in the community of people who speak our new language, day in and day out. Measures of investment like these form the foundation of our language intelligence.

Creative Expression

Learning language is less about efficiency, and more about memorability.

I recall the first time I shared my testimony in another language. I was sitting in a taxi in Bangkok, Thailand with a sheet of notebook paper in my hand. On the sheet was scribbled about ten sentences that somebody had translated for me earlier that morning. I recited it over and over until I had memorized it. I tried to make it sound fluent. After some "taxi talk", I asked if I could tell a story. I held the paper in front of me and raced through all ten sentences, barely taking a breath. My taxi driver patiently asked me to say it again, only this time in my own words, so he could understand me. I learned a valuable lesson that day about the importance of presenting the gospel in a person's heart language, from the heart.

There is a big difference between saying something that we've memorized and putting together phrases and sentences in creative and meaningful ways with words we know. Both communicate a message, but one sounds rote – because it is – while the other is truly generated from our own thoughts. Language is not simply stacks of memorized phrases. It's not like we're building with Lego. Language is generative, interactive. One simple phrase, like a living cell, can reproduce into a thousand other expressions.

> One simple phrase, like a living cell, can reproduce into a thousand other expressions.

Basic language skill development means we create and build onto meaningful communication foundations that are simple in structure, yet generative in nature. The natural process of learning a language begins with the use of simple words which form and grow into meaningful phrases, short and simple sentences which grow into complex sentences and structures, and simple familiar-themed paragraphs which grow into complete stories and discourses. Most significantly, it is the centrifugal force of regular and varied conversations we have with lots of people in the language that promotes this growth. This is when we reach a level of *basic conversational fluency*, our first step toward *gospel fluency*.

So how do we reach *basic conversational fluency*? In other words, how do we move from being mentally tethered to strings of memorized phrases and into this world of creative expression? It all starts with memorability.

Our minds are wonderfully able to remember things, to capture new data in a moment, and move it from the temporary storage of complex cognitive information – *working memory* – to the storage and retrieval of information beyond the initial few seconds – *long-term associative memory*. We do this all the time when we want to remember things – something someone said, a phone number, words to a song. And we do this deliberately and consistently when we review notes for a class or study for a test.

If we don't practice recall with regular review, we tend to forget. The dark line on the graph is the *Forgetting Curve* which represents what happens when we fail to exercise our ability to remember things. We forget almost everything we do not consciously try to remember.

Forgetting Curve

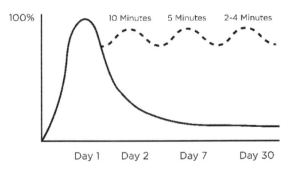

The dashed line on the graph represents the application of *spaced learning*. Spaced learning is a method through which content is repeated or reviewed several times, deliberately interspersed with diversions and activities including rest and sleep. The practice of spaced learning helps us remember better and more easily.

Strategic-repetition practices like spaced learning are designed to get shorter and easier with each successive review. Consistent review minimizes the carnage of our poor memory practices by helping us practice associations and create better long-term memory storage. "Our memories are vast interlocking webs of data. They are like thick robust branches, and more and thicker branches means easier recall."[14]

Memories connect with our senses. We see them, hear them, feel, them, taste them, even smell them. Memories have meaning and personal relevance. We always have some sort of emotional attachment to our memories. We are able to, in a sense, relive our memories. We can, with practice, experience some memories as if we were in the moment. In other words, our minds actually have the capacity, at least to some extent, to re-activate our working memory by reliving long-term memories that just need more reinforcement. "Every time we recall information from long-term storage into working memory, we re-learn it."[15]

We can learn to apply this as we learn our new language, by attaching words and phrases to meaningful and sensory-driven experiences we re-live with our language partners. We may have shared-stories that we tell again and again, stories that bring up sensory-driven memories and feelings.

This is especially helpful with familiar stories that have deep and personal meaning to us, such as gospel stories. We have so much texture with which to remember these in a new language when we listen to them and learn to re-tell them.

As described, our brains are good at grouping things that seem to go together. We do this naturally by association, which is all a part of our memory process. We more easily remember groups of things, like kitchen utensils, or furniture items.

This is also helpful for combining words, phrases, and sentences into whole ideas. If we know the words, and meaningful combinations of them, our brains will prefer the meaning of the entire topic, rarely focusing on the meaning of individual words.

This represents the art and practice of creative expression. Related, when we speak *extemporaneously*, we are allowing the topic or thought to reside in our brains as we try to communicate the ideas through the creative combination of words. We may even have notes, but our focus is on the meaning. The words are free flowing, the discourse cohesive. It has the feel of being prepared, but not polished; vigorous, yet flexible, adaptable to the context.

We need to do our best to interpret our fluency of expression in light of the message we intend to communicate. Our goal is primarily not form or skill development, rather communicating our message clearly, accurately, and naturally. The practice of creative expression therefore takes our focus from the details and places it squarely on communicating the message, so that the details can take their place. Our simple creative personal stories have the capacity to invite us into the lives of our neighbors – even taxi drivers – in meaningful and powerful ways that may just open the door to the gospel.

Immersion

Immersion is a second-by-second decision to die to self and come alive to the new language and culture God has called us to. It is being with people, in the moment, not just passing time with people in a place.[16]

Immersion, measured in moments of relational and language focus, constitutes an inherent investment in the lives of people around us, as we learn their language. The single most important thing we can do to learn the language is spend deliberate time with people using the language. Immersion is the essential choice to engage.

Immersion is measured in nano-seconds.

The practice of language immersion is less about mechanics and more about attitude. Immersion in a speech community, in a geographic sense, is a myth. Many of us can be literally surrounded by the language, yet never really immerse. We can remain disconnected, orbiting the culture, never fully engaging. The abundance of English, non-local communities, work responsibilities, or even just a part-time learner mindset can set into motion an overwhelming tide that pushes us away from the language and culture.

Immersion actually starts by surrounding ourselves with language we are able to comprehend including basic greetings, survival expressions, routine instructions, and simple descriptions. From the day we start learning a new language, we can begin to engage, respond, and experience what it means to immerse. Surrounding ourselves with language that we can understand, or getting abundant doses of *comprehensible input*, is one of the most powerful immersion practices we can experience. On both a technical and relational level, immersion really does start with listening to what we understand.

But it doesn't stop there. One of the most powerful principles of *comprehensible input* is that our exposure to the language we understand actually creates a thirst for more, and we can build on this as we immerse ourselves in reasonably secure communication environments, such as our time spent with language partners. Immersive moments with the intention to learn create ideal settings for adding small amounts of new language input to larger amounts of comprehensible input, thus expanding our comprehension, and therefore enhancing our immersion.

I am inspired by learners who have the tenacity to zero-in on immersion opportunities even in the most unsuspecting places and settings. Just being in a place with people who speak a certain language does not necessarily mean we are immersed. Nor does having one-on-one conversations with Russian speakers in New York City mean we are not immersed.

> Immersion has never been less a matter of geography than it is today. Immersion is no longer measured in GPS coordinates. We cannot assume that our presence within a speech community naturally leads to language practice. Rather, immersion is defined by choices we make at any given moment to engage with people in their language, the language we are learning.[17]

There are very few spaces in our rapidly urbanizing world where the practice of immersion in specific speech communities remains a limited option. People are literally everywhere! Students who find opportunities to immerse themselves in the language for six months to a year can often reach conversational ability in their new language before they even leave home.

Imagine having the ability to converse on basic topics in the language upon arrival to a new location! Our entire entry experience at that point would springboard to a whole new level. I've heard this described as arriving to a new place with some friends: grammar friends, vocabulary friends, comprehension friends, and overall confidence-building friends. This is what we mean by putting strategy into practice, well before arrival. This is an example of intelligent language investment.

On one occasion Jesus sent his disciples on a journey instructing them, "Take nothing for the road," he told them, "no staff, no traveling bag, no bread, no money; and don't take an extra shirt" (Luke 9:3).

We need to shed false dependencies when we enter our new culture. By God's grace we should aim to use only our new language upon arrival and depend on the help we receive in the language from sympathetic friends and new neighbors. "In our first 72 hours we should not be allowed to rely on anything in our own language."[18]

Does this sound crazy? It's not. It's actually one of the most powerful and intelligent things we can do as we enter a new language environment, setting into motion new ways of thinking, relating, and doing things. "After a week, as we learn to live in our city, our mindsets shift. We are no longer afraid to engage."[19] Fear is a powerful motivator. So is courage.

The insanity of the first 72 hours, even the first week, can push against our efforts to immerse. Immersion is a huge effort and there's a lot of resistance. Just setting it up can be challenging, and a big "sell" for people to get on board. We may be neither able to muster much sentiment within us nor around us to prioritize immersion plans over the logistics of life that seem so critical at the time. Sometimes the two just don't work well together.

If our focus remains only on getting ready to live, we will generally orient our lives toward the expediency of our life needs, overshadowing and sometimes entirely quenching the intentionality of our language needs, which are always less urgent, but arguably more important, for long-term cross-cultural fruitfulness. Some life choices may seem smart on the front end, but in the final analysis may actually hinder our reaching fluency in the language and culture. "Getting ready to live and getting ready to learn are two very different things."[20]

When we enter a new language setting we immediately enter the apprenticeship of one or another language orientation: either English, or our new language. For most of us, for myriad reasons, our default expression, our apprenticeship, will be toward English, unless we are very intentional in our daily orientation. "We don't need a blanket of English surrounding the new language we are trying to use."[21]

I'm convinced that as newcomers [enter] a culture with the kind of orientation that puts a focus on relationships, [they] can get deeply involved in very, very meaningful relationships, and they not only can, but must do it from the very first day, right from the outset. If they don't, then they're just going to be tourists.[22]

The choice to immerse is not easy. It's intentional. It's hard. Many of us well-intentioned learners all too often find ourselves in the comfort zone of English when we should be in the immersive growth zone of our new language. This is because honestly there's not much that is immediately gratifying when we are constantly swimming underwater in the new expressions and cultural nuances, trying to catch a breath of sanity. There is truly a lot about language immersion that can just make us tired and frustrated. Therefore, it is always helpful when we can remind ourselves, or even better when someone else can remind us, that our choice to immerse in the language is not just an intelligent language choice, but it's also an obedient and ultimately, deeply fulfilling choice, one that resonates with our call, as we begin to experience the joy of sharing the gospel with our dear neighbors.

Chapter Summary

- The practice of intelligent language learning starts with investing in creative expression and immersion.

Reflect and Respond

1. Consider this statement: *Our personal LQ or "language intelligence" has far less to do with cognitive aptitude and far more to do with our power to discover and harness language resources we all have within us and around us.* What is one way you can improve your LQ?

   _____

   _____

   _____

2. Describe how you plan to reach *basic conversational fluency* in your new language.

   _____

   _____

   _____

3. Consider this statement: *Immersion is the essential choice to engage.* What is one way you can adjust your life to better immerse yourselves in the language among those who speak it?

   _____

   _____

   _____

4. Respond to this statement: *"In our first 72 hours we should not be allowed to rely on anything in our own language."* How would you envision your first 72 hours? For example, how would you prepare for it?

_____

_____

_____

My Next Faithful Step

Describe one way you resolve to put what you have learned from Chapter 7 *LQ* into practice.

_____

_____

_____

For more about how to start well in your new language read *From Zero to Basic Conversational Fluency* and *Twelve Weeks to Basic Conversational Fluency* (article and lessons) found at www.language180.com or just use the QR code found at the introduction and conclusion of the book.

8

Deep and Wide

Goal: Invest in life-long language learning.

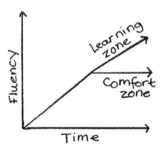

I will not be content until I can minister in [my new language] similar to how I would be able to in English. I know this is a lofty goal. But the gospel, as well as deep spiritual truths and doctrines, best communicates in the heart language of a people. I firmly believe this. This is what drives me. (Sam— second year language learner.)

An international partner and I were talking with a national who used a phrase neither of us understood. We both caught the context and the conversation continued to flow but at one point my partner asked, "You know that phrase you used a minute ago to describe..." and we both were able to learn a new idiom. I was particularly impressed with the in-language tempo of his question and how it just seemed to fit within the conversation.

After another conversation I saw him pull out his dictionary and write in his notebook. The surprising thing about all of this is that this guy's language is great, well past the level where most of us would say we've learned "enough" to do our work. He has a fruitful ministry in the language, and I sense that his lifelong learning posture contributes to this. I asked him about his language, why he kept learning, and what it's done for him.

- He regularly prayed with local friends and ministered to them from God's word in the language.

- He did his personal devotions in the language.

- He digested books, articles, news, and other media to stay informed, improve expression, and develop precision.

- He took notes, kept a journal, prepared lessons, and taught in the language, regularly reviewing all of this with work and ministry partners.

- He described the joy of evangelizing the lost, discipling new believers, and training church leaders; and the practice of always improving his language to become better at doing these things.

I was inspired to hear my friend share both how and why he relentlessly pushed himself to continue learning. I was also humbled. We need to ask ourselves: are we inspired to continue learning, or are we content with mediocre language? Will we continue learning, or are we content to remain at a place where we are barely able to teach the gospel in our new language?

Sadly, there is a strong tendency for people to just remain shallow and narrow in their new language. But I have good news! We can continue to improve. We can dig deeper, and we can reach wider. I exhort us to regularly answer to these very real and relevant questions as we pursue *gospel fluency*:

> How wide is my language?
> How deep is my language?

What can I do today to reach out just a little bit further, to understand my neighbors just a little bit better; their families, their communities, and how they do life?

Concentric Circles to Widen our Language

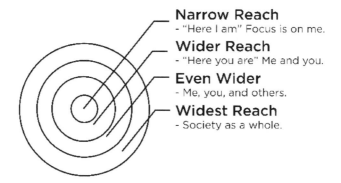

How can I reach in just a little bit more, to probe a little deeper, to understand what makes my neighbors afraid, or sad, or to find out what they dream of, or hope for?

Concentric Circles to Deepen our Language

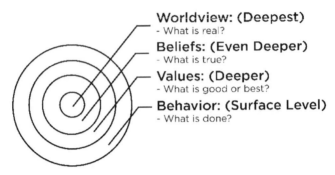

Worldview: (Deepest)
- What is real?

Beliefs: (Even Deeper)
- What is true?

Values: (Deeper)
- What is good or best?

Behavior: (Surface Level)
- What is done?

As we dive deeper and wider in our language learning there are significant barriers that may keep us from doing this. Below are top-ten barriers commonly preventing learners from going deep and wide in the language. There are also ongoing learning practices that require our deliberate effort to push us beyond our comfort zone, into deeper and wider zones of learning. Below are also top-ten practices that can help us stay in our learning zone.

Barrier #1: Lack of Vision

Fundamental to our success in language learning is the understanding that we are not called to learn the language, we are called to proclaim the gospel. We have no other reason to learn the language. At the same time, we have every reason to learn the language well, in order to be able to proclaim the gospel fluently. Language learning is relevant to in-language ministry. Always. So often, for any number of reasons, we can lose sight of the relevance of our language progress in ministry. When we cannot clearly see the direct ministry relevance of our language practice and progress, or even when the relevance clouds over for some reason, we can lose momentum in our learning. Language learning is a long-term commitment that is often a challenge to sustain without a clear and long-term vision.

Barrier #2: Part-Time Learner Mindset

We make the mistake of approaching learning a language as we would a job or a class. This "part-time learner" mindset cripples our progress. We may even commit to 30 "full-time" hours each week, while still maintaining this unhealthy mindset. Hours clocked or semester credits earned mean little if we are still unable to sustain a meaningful conversation with our neighbors.

A friend once told me that language is not just a thing we learn, rather it's a life we live. A healthy language mindset is less about hours and test scores and more about momentum, traction, immersion, and investment in the relationships with neighbors who speak the language. Do we use what language we know when we meet with neighbors? Do we talk to ourselves in the language? Do we ever dream in our new language?

A part-time learning mindset can kill momentum. Sure, we can crunch the numbers to predict that with our half-time language we'll eventually get there, it'll just take twice as long. Sadly, more often than not we just find ourselves making negligible if any real progress. But if we start strong, we may just surprise ourselves by capturing a momentum that helps us to sustain a "new normal" even when we are forced to cut back on hours: chatting in the language for a few minutes with a co-worker over coffee, adding a few bedtime stories in the language to read to the kids at night, creating social media spaces in the language that invite us into new friendships.

Barrier #3: English-Dominant Identity

For many of us, work and life responsibilities pull us away from opportunities to learn and use the language. We end up spending so much of our daily lives in English. Meetings, travel, and electronic communication present huge challenges to those of us wanting to make progress. Those of us in urban areas may find ourselves surrounded (distracted? tempted?) by malls, international organizations (usually in English), apps, social media, TV, internet, and countless life circles representing entire English-dominant ecosystems threatening our language progress. Instead of finding ways to mitigate these challenges, we can become comfortable in our expat lifestyles and identities.

Those of us with heavy work-related responsibilities in English should seriously consider investing an up-front three-months in a full-immersion language experience before ever taking on normal workloads. Doing so will at least bring us within range of basic conversational fluency and hopefully generate the traction we need to keep growing in the language despite limited immersion experiences.

Barrier #4: Ridicule from Nationals and Co-workers

Unsympathetic criticism, ridicule, or even casual indifference from people who have high influence in our new language lives – usually colleagues and national partners – can literally shut us down, crushing our efforts to make progress. We need all the encouragement we can get, bucket loads in fact, and from the right people. Local language partners, ministry partners, and colleagues are the *single most influential people* in our new language lives. Their support matters! Negative criticism, ridicule, or even just leaving our efforts ignored can be powerfully demoralizing for those of us aspiring to learn the language, who simply need a word of encouragement that the rigorous and faithful language practices we apply are yielding the fruit of godly ministry.

Barrier #5: Lack of Team Support

Some of us may have mentors or supervisors who do not encourage us in language progress. This is especially true if they, too, are struggling in their language or culture acquisition, don't see the need, or consider it a waste of time. We may have people with whom we work who discourage us simply because of their lack of interest or progress.

One of the most encouraging things learners can hear are testimonies from co-workers of fruitful in-language experiences. People around us are making progress and God is at work, and we need to hear this! When we don't have opportunities to share or hear these great stories, we can lose momentum in our own progress.

We need to have greater transparency on teams when it comes to learning and using our new language in life and ministry. In a recent conversation with language coaches, several talked about leaders and more experienced colleagues they knew and worked with who extended sincere efforts to sympathize with struggling language learners. In place of negative comparisons and shame, they chose to create healthy spaces for dialogue about language needs, and even sought to practice the language together.

Every team should have some sort of "no shame" policy to encourage the use of the language with each other. I'm not talking about formal lessons, scripts, and certainly nothing evaluative, rather a common practice that praises and encourages a pursuit of *gospel fluency* for all – through furious resolve, and profound humility. I don't know how else to say it: We just need the attitude of Christ to permeate our teams (Philippians 2:5).

Jenn and Lauren have coffee together each week for accountability and prayer. Every other week they enjoy using only their new language as they converse and pray together. Jenn is more fluent, but is patient with Lauren, who is an eager and able learner.

Scott and Rick meet with a national disciple. Scott starts off reading and talking through a few verses. Rick, more experienced in the language, picks up from where Scott leaves off. Each week, Scott gets better and contributes more.

A couple of singles at the end of their first year on the field meet for lunch with their team leader to talk about how things are going. They decide to have the whole conversation in Russian.

Barrier #6: No Close Relationships with Nationals

Lack of exposure to the language is one thing, but the lack of affirming and supportive relationships with nationals is quite another and can seriously diminish our efforts to make progress. We make time for people who are important to us. Until our neighbors become important to us, we won't make time for them. We need to constantly evaluate our priorities as we relate to our neighbors. Learners who spend time with nationals generally make progress. Learners who don't, generally won't.

Our oldest son Jake spent a year at boarding school in another country. He took a language class, but mostly just spent time meeting and conversing with neighbors in order to learn the language. One day while shopping he dropped a ring that rolled under the rack. After trying to make himself understood by the clerk he did the next best thing and asked some guys walking by who helped him not only recover the ring but learn to say, "move the rack" and "find the ring" in his new language.

I can risk 10 minutes of awkwardness for a potential lifetime of friendship. (Jake Fidler)

As international Christian workers we tend to rely largely on paid relationships with nationals, truncating our language acquisition, cultural awareness, and interpersonal growth. We need relationships with nationals, lots of them, and need to invest time with them in order to sustain healthy growth in our cultural understanding and awareness. Bill, a second-year learner, shared with me these wise insights he recently learned from a national brother.

> I had a long talk with our national ministry partner about what it means to be a good worker. His two exhortations were to: 1) Know the culture better than you know the language and as good as you know the Bible and 2) Make the local church feel responsibility for itself. He also gave several examples from his years of ministry partnership with foreigners and it has helped give me a goal to shoot for.

Barrier #7: Excessive Social Media and Virtual Ghettos

Social media has created a global trend substituting virtual relationships over in-person relationships, which can have a strong negative effect on our language progress. Virtual communities tend to assume a life of their own and can distract us from daily face-to-face conversations that provide us the interaction so essential to sustain and improve our interpersonal language skills. The sheer volume of screen time we habitually engage in may actually rob us of the precious conversation time we need to have with neighbors. We may just need to turn off our phones.

Barrier #8: Intangible Destabilizers

Frustration, fatigue, embarrassment, stage fright, culture shock, and culture stress can all serve to weaken our resolve and throw us off balance in our learning progress. These toxic intangible destabilizers have the potential to really sabotage our learning.

We may find ourselves surrounded by social situations we struggle to understand, which make us feel negatively evaluated and perhaps misunderstood by those around us in our new lives. This kind of stress can literally rob us of our physical and emotional health.

When we face these kinds of stressful evaluative situations in our new language life, which for most of us is a daily challenge, we need to be aware of the dangers they pose and find ways to overcome these extreme language barriers.

Barrier #9: Family Considerations and Challenges

Those of us who have experienced trying to balance learning the language while raising small children or negotiating their educational needs understand the true meaning of time and energy scarcity. We need all the help we can get to really make it work. Spouses may have different learning needs. Children have needs. Families need to work with these challenging dynamics to find ways to make progress. As fathers, we need to watch our kids. As husbands, we need to help our wives get the time they need to learn the language. I've seen first-hand how easy it is for a mother to experience the crushing stress of daily trauma from when the doorbell rings, to when someone says something to her kids, or when someone just tries to talk with her on the street in passing, and she doesn't know the language.

Our families should never be barriers to our learning the language. Let's celebrate the huge blessing and value our family identities bring into our new language and culture settings! God is intimately aware of our family situations and he cares for us, and for our families, whether those in our immediate homes (spouses and children), relatives, churches, or even those on our teams. These special relationships are a vibrant part of our family identities and testify to God's goodness and the gospel in our lives.

Barrier #10: Getting Stuck on the Mediocre Plateau

Mediocrity may be enough for many life skills, maybe even enough to "get by" in our new language, but it's not enough if we really want to clearly communicate the gospel to our neighbors. We need to continue learning, and to find ways to rise above the *language plateau*.

Pursuing any skill development, (and language is no exception), we may imagine that given enough time we continue to improve toward mastery (see the *Imagined Learning Curve* graph). In reality, when we reach "good enough" we hit a cognitive plateau in our learning, (see the *Language Plateau* graph). Whether it's typing, reading, playing an instrument, or learning a language, we are hard-wired to reach a level of basic autonomous proficiency that we often call *mediocrity*, just enough ability to "get by" with ease in just about any skill, and then we simply stop improving.

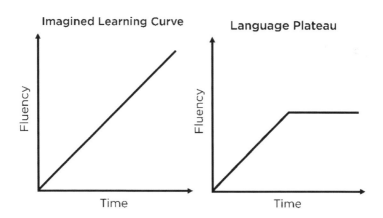

Our learning paths may resemble the following two charts describing what often happens when we reach a *basic conversational fluency* (BCF) breakthrough point where our language is good enough to get by and we are tempted to coast. It's at that point we have two paths from which to choose: one of deliberate and ongoing progress (into our learning zone) or one of plateauing (remaining in our comfort zone), illustrated by the *Learning Zone vs Comfort Zone* chart.

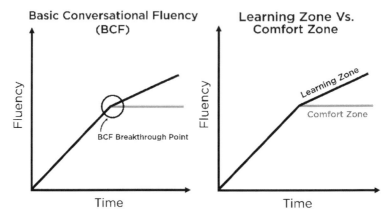

The path to mastery in the *learning zone* is very challenging. We will inevitably face increasing and very real obstacles of diminishing returns. High-frequency words that once came to us in easy-to-create sentences are now the less-frequent words, nuanced meanings, abstract concepts, technical terms, and challenging complex structures that take more time and energy to master with seemingly fewer and slower tangible results.

We may be tempted to stop growing, perhaps even subconsciously, and before we know it, we may find ourselves coasting for months or even years. What we need to realize is the road to continued language growth beyond the *breakthrough point* of *basic conversational fluency* is a deliberate choice, a conscious effort. We must *choose* to stay in the *language learning zone*.

We have to work hard to reach basic proficiency at any skill, but we have to work even harder to become really good at that skill. Language is no exception. Operating in the language learning zone means far more than simply autonomously using what we already know. Rather, it means cognitively moving forward into learning what we do not yet know. This literally means we push ourselves to failure, the kind of failure that fuels a will to find a way to correct our mistakes and try again until we experience improvement. In this learning zone we need to view things and do things differently, perhaps like never before. And we also need endurance, perhaps like never before. But it's also where we experience tremendous joy, because this is where we begin to experience ministry opportunities in the language like never before.

When we are in the language learning zone, we find that we get to share the gospel with our neighbors more often, in more life contexts, and from more scriptures than ever before. This is that healthy and thriving path of ongoing learning where we can truly dive deep and wide into our language and ministry. The way to get on this path, and stay in this zone, is by immediately beginning to apply healthy language learning zone practices.

Learning Zone Practice #1: The Familiar Discomfort of Immersion

Breaking my normal routine and doing something out of the ordinary is at first discomforting. But then it becomes a "familiar discomfort" which is do-able. (Will, first-year learner)

The main reason we resist immersing into a new place and culture, with new people in a new language, is because it's uncomfortable. We don't ever naturally seek discomfort. We have to intentionally pursue it. We have to break old routines and create new ones. That's how it works for Will, who goes to the same place, to meet the same people, often at the same time, when he's practicing his language. This at least creates a familiarity that he can move toward as a "familiar discomfort."

It's within these familiar zones, Will goes on to say, that people come alongside him. "It's refreshing to know I have a time and place I can anticipate, to be able to talk with people in my new language, within my new culture."

The connection is important. Will has made friends, so he doesn't feel alone in this immersion experience. "It's easier to do this with your friends. This makes the outside-of-my-comfort-zone experience more relaxing, enjoyable, and refreshing. I no longer focus on how nervous I am, and I can focus on what's going on" (Will).

Learning Zone Practice #2: Making Space for Creative Expression

> *When I work on my speech, I create a mental space that is separate from everything else. And when I practice it, I enter that mental space. This is my memory zone, my mental zone. (Eric, first-year learner)*

Creating language requires mental space and this almost always requires a dedicated time with dedicated partners. When we begin to create in the language by putting words together into hundreds and thousands of meaningful phrases and sentences, we need space for experimentation, trial and error, thinking about new words and combinations of words, remembering things we learn, mentally categorizing them, talking to ourselves; writing, talking, re-writing, and re-talking. We need a safe place where we can say things over and over again from our notes and from our memories, and where we can receive immediate, constructive, and positive feedback from proficient speakers so we can do it all over again, only better, the next time.

Learning Zone Practice #3: The Art of Failing, and Getting Immediate Feedback

Linguistic breakdown is the road to growth.
(MT, co-worker)

Regular practice simply isn't enough to improve; we must watch ourselves fail, practice failing, and get feedback on how to improve. Until we see the incredible value of failing – that is, pushing ourselves into areas of needed growth, where failure leads to analysis, adjustment, and change – we will not improve.

High performing language learners celebrate every small victory, and literally measure even the most incremental points of success, especially those that emerge from failure. High performing language learners study themselves failing and have the will to continue improving past the point where most people plateau. Unlike perfectionists, who often obsessively (and often paralyzingly) pursuing flawless performance, high performers are simply not content with average ability, identify *specific* points of weakness, work on them, and steadily improve.

Learning Zone Practice #4: Expanding the Language We Need

People will only learn the language they need.[23]

We may need to re-engineer our lives so that we put ourselves in situations where we need more language. We cannot measure what we learn by what we want to learn. We measure what we learn by what we need to learn. Sure, we may want to improve, but unless what we want becomes what we need, we won't learn what we want. If we want to improve, we must change the language we need and put ourselves into positions and situations where we need more than we have.

"It's hard to continue to get the language you want, after you already have the language you need."[24]

Don is an excellent teacher of Old Testament. I love hearing him teach in the language. He has great language. I asked him what he did to reach this level. He arrived years ago as an English teacher and reached reasonable conversational fluency. Then he was invited to teach Old Testament and that was all it took for him to work hard to be able to teach it in the language. Don prepared lessons and then practiced them over and over again until he was able to fluently teach them.

Learning Zone Practice #5: Scaffolding

When we are in over-our-heads, we get the language we need.[25]

When my boys were kids, they practiced backflips as I spotted them with my hands. Soon, they were doing backflips on their own without my *scaffolding*. But they probably never would have attempted backflips without a little help.

We must find effective ways to move from un-deliberate usage to deliberate practice, from using language we are comfortable with, to using language just out of our range. This is a recipe for failure without some sort of scaffolding; someone there to help us work on new language, to help us understand it, and eventually master it. Scaffolding creates a space, a zone, for this kind of growth. We need to do whatever we can to create these spaces where we can freely and safely practice new content, forms, and usages with sympathetic language partners. Scaffolded conversations are more intense than most normal conversations we have with our neighbors.

I recently experienced this at a sports medicine workshop I attended in my new language where our instructor, Denise, used a form of scaffolding called a *teach-back*. For each set of instructions, she would stop and say, "Okay, now you do it," and we each would take turns while she observed us and corrected us as needed. After a few false starts, we were usually all able to work through the instructions and activities with reasonable success. First, we watched, then practiced, then were finally able to actually teach each other the intended outcomes, performing the desired tasks with reasonable success and confidence.

Denise taught us fluently in her new language. I asked her how she had reached such fluency. Not surprisingly, she described learning language in the same way she taught our workshop. Whenever she had something she needed to say, whether it was something in the field of sports medicine or something from the Bible, she would prepare it and present it, mistakes and all, to someone willing to listen to her and willing to provide helpful feedback in the form of a *teachback*. Denise made it her job to then close the distance between what she could already do in the language, and what she had just learned. In this way, Denise created a path to fluency in her new language, and so can we.

Learning Zone Practice #6: Dual Investment

It is very hard to be both accurate and fluent at the same time.[26]

Some of our most fruitful advanced language practices are those special times when we can work on fluency and accuracy together, at the same time. Typically, in everyday speech, we use the same content with the same usages and though our language flows, it does not necessarily improve. Then in formal learning settings, we often receive an abundance of formal instruction which may not be readily useful in our daily lives. We tend to oscillate between these two extremes from using what we know and not improving, to learning new things that we cannot readily apply. What we need is a healthy combination of both, a *dual-investment* zone to help us focus on *what* we want to communicate (the content and meaning), as well as *how* we should learn to communicate it (accurately, naturally, and clearly) at the same time.

Not long ago, I heard a friend ask his language partner, "What happens after you die?" What followed was an incredibly interesting discussion about the meaning and use of the word *disappear,* unlocking tremendous insights into beliefs about the afterlife, what is real, what is not, how we exist in this form, and how one day we will not, and how the use of the words – like *disappear* – can be so perplexing, yet so enlightening.

We can also practice speaking by switching roles. My friend's language partner could have asked him, "What happens after you die?" After a lively discussion, and a recording, we as learners could then ask, "What did I say correctly?" Or "What did I say incorrectly?" Or even, "How could I have said this better or differently?"

So, as we practice the discussion – for example, talking about what happens after we die – we are also learning the grammar and usages of words such as *disappear*. As we talk about the content, we are also learning new endings, and new ways to say things better. The more we massage the words and texts, the richer our learning will be with each encounter.

Learning Zone Practice #7: "Just in Time" Learning (Minimizing and Optimizing)

Sometimes less is more.

Not all language investment is created equal. We may spend hours and hours in activities that don't get us very far or learn more in just half an hour of solid effective investment. How do we measure the quality our language time? How can we get the most out of our investment? On a scale of 1-10, how can we stay in the 8-10 range in our strategies and practice? How can we detect and adjust what we are doing, for example, if we find ourselves in the 5-6 range? What does that even mean? Precisely this: We need to practice the right program or activity of learning at the right time, for the right amount of time, with the right people. In other words, we need to learn to be innovative and eclectic in our approaches to language learning so that we find what works for us when we need it, in exact measure and distribution. We need to practice "just-in-time" learning.

> There's a big difference between what we know
> and what we need at three months and six months
> of learning. (JH, co-worker)

We need to capture those teachable moments when we need new grammar structures or vocabulary, so that we learn them effectively and use them immediately. In other words, we need to learn the language we need, when we need it. That may sound simple enough, but sadly, many of us are notoriously tempted to fill hours and notebooks with grammar rules and charts we cannot begin to effectively put into practice at that time. Instead, we just need clear, relevant instruction about how to use the language we need, when we need it.

> When you want to get good at something, how you
> spend your time practicing is far more important than
> the amount of time you spend. In fact, in every domain
> of expertise that's been rigorously examined, from
> chess to violin to basketball, studies have found that the
> number of years one has been doing something
> correlates only weakly with level of performance.[27]

Our early language is about meeting our immediate needs within our immediate environment. This may include descriptions, commands, or instructions that apply the use of very basic words and phrases, using simple grammar. Trying to learn more complex forms at this point would be premature and counterproductive if we cannot yet describe what is before us (literally), engage in basic conversations, or talk about what we did yesterday. Our language learning zone is dynamic and can be best described as those *best practices* which fit well within our optimal zone for that season of learning, that day, that hour, and even that moment.

Learning Zone Practice #8: The Rhythm of Endurance

Run the mile you're in. (Ryan Hall, Olympic Marathoner)

Scott approached me to ask if I could help him arrange a language sprint. I'd never even heard of a language sprint! He described it as a burst of extreme language intensity for a specified amount of time (usually a few weeks) to infuse his language progress. He needed to do something to jumpstart his language and wanted to give this idea a try.

Scott had spent years learning language for more effective ministry in his community. He exemplified an effective ongoing learning rhythm he described as the "life-long learner's posture" which he applied to his ministry practice. I love that concept. Scott never stopped learning, because the more language he learned, the better he could minister to his neighbors.

Scott then moved to a global city which took him out of his ministry language for a season. With a heavy travel and training schedule, and limited access to his ministry language and community, Scott could have taken a language break, but he didn't. As he prayed, the Lord led Scott to a community of unreached immigrants in the city from my part of the world who spoke the language I knew. I was thrilled as Scott began to learn their language and share the gospel with them. Scott was making progress and engaging in fruitful conversations, but it was definitely slow-going. With many other responsibilities, Scott had to make a strong effort to invest in the language and community with what little time he had.

After several months of limited progress, Scott and I began to put together his sprint, a four-week adventure that would include 60 weekly hours of intense, eclectic activities designed to push him to the brink of his language capacity, and then maybe a little bit more.

We knew this would not be a sustainable learning pace but hoped he could manage it for a month. Scott's goals included: infusing his language with floods of fluency practice, nailing down some basic accuracy issues, overcoming some psychological plateaus brought on by the slow progress, and reorienting his learning posture so he could better engage his neighbors in his new language.

Scott spent the first three-weeks in my neighborhood. I barely saw him, but when I did, I could tell he was really pushing hard and making great progress. He was definitely getting tired but hanging in there. Scott arranged to spend his final week with his neighbor from his city who had returned to his hometown for a holiday. Honored to have Scott in his home, and proud of his improved language, Scott's neighbor did what most of my neighbors here do as he introduced him to everyone in the community as his guest which prompted many invitations to hours and hours of tea, conversation, and life in the neighborhood.

At the end of four weeks, Scott was tired, but fulfilled. He returned to his city having reached his goals. A week or two later I asked Scott if he had any surprising take-aways. He described that while the sprint had predictably helped him learn more language and engage at deeper and broader levels, it had unexpectedly helped him create a "new normal" for his learning and ministry practices in the language. The intensity of Scott's sprint seemed to ignite motivation and infuse a freshness into the day-in and day-out rhythm of his learning and ministry in the city. This helped Scott continue to make good progress in his language and overcome challenging routines.

As a life-long learner Scott continues to exemplify what it means to create a healthy "rhythm of endurance" while he presses on in his language practice. I love the title of Ryan Hall's new book *Run the Mile You're In: Finding God in Every Step* (Zondervan, 2019). We can learn a lot from the guy who reached the pinnacle of elite distance running with God as his coach. I've heard language learning described as a marathon, not a sprint. But it's really both, isn't it? For Scott, one doesn't come without the other.

Learning Zone Practice #9: Demystifying Progress

What do I need to do to move forward? (Mel, first-year learner)

We as learners have a stake in our language progress. Language policy for many sending organizations may articulate minimum level requirements as a starting point for effective ministry. Sadly, many of us often see this as a final level to reach, and nothing more. What prevents us from seeing the need to continue learning beyond minimum standards, to master fluency toward more fruitful ministry outcomes? How can we see beyond the enforcement of policy and begin to own the evaluation process of our personal language and ministry progress toward reaching *gospel fluency*?

Is it possible for us to reorient our perspective of language levels, viewing our proficiency not as a point or level, rather as the dynamic of what we can do, and what we cannot yet do, in both breadth and depth of expression, so that we can find a path forward? Are we willing and able to take that next step, our next language assignment, whatever it may be, and begin to seriously align it with our overall calling and purpose?

This week I was able to share the story in Mark 2:1-12 with my teacher. I shared with her three examples from the story, all relating to Jesus being God. Without preparing that passage I would not have been able to explain it so clearly. She asked some good questions. It was neat because God used an assignment to share gospel truths with my teacher. (Karen, first-year learner)

I love this perspective! This week Karen was able to make measurable progress in her language. This tells me Karen made it her goal to share this story from the Gospel of Mark. This was an assignment that she created for herself. No one else told her to do this. Karen made it her goal to share three examples all relating to Jesus as God. This defined her path of learning, guided her preparation, and helped her see truth in her new language in a new light which she was able to then share with her teacher.

I am a strong advocate for creating smart goals like these for every two weeks of our learning as we pursue *gospel fluency*. This is a great way to get feedback, as we saw Karen do with her teacher, and then monitor or track that feedback. This creates a personal history of progress and a veritable roadmap to fluency, providing a healthy and clear perspective for what we have done, what we are able to do, and informing us where and how we need to move forward with confidence and success.

When we, as learners, create our own personal progress history – that is, when we create regular and frequent goals, aspire and work hard to reach those goals, and create an environment where we can regularly present the outcomes of those goals for immediate feedback and clarity of progress – we can then more readily see how our documented and current language journey fits into the greater *gospel fluency* picture.

Learning Zone Practice #10: Envisioning

> I will not be content until I can minister in [my new language] similar to how I would be able to in English. I know this is a lofty goal. But the gospel, as well as deep spiritual truths and doctrines, best communicate in the heart language of a people. I firmly believe this. This is what drives me. (Sam, second-year learner)

Sam's perspective represents vision. We always need to keep the vision of our language and calling before us. The best way I can explain or describe this is simply through the words of learners who relentlessly and faithfully practice this.

> I need to be grounded in the Word of God in their language. My language has to be at a place where I can take them to the Word of God, that my hunger for the Word is contagious, so they hunger and search for the things that deeply satisfy their souls, suffering, and pain. (Alice, diaspora worker)

Alice works with displaced peoples who have experienced great trauma and continue to suffer in ways we can hardly even imagine. She has entered into their lives, using their language, to listen, empathize, and share the eternal hope and great comfort of the gospel. She can only do this with great language.

> Language learning is one of the hardest things I've ever done. What was the game changer for me? I had "hard language" with no "ministry joy." It was torture. But when I found ministry joy in the hard language progress, it was no longer torture. It was rewarding. (Greg, first-year learner)

Greg began to experience the joy of language learning once he began to see the purpose in a new light, one that ushered him to enter into ministry while using the language. Even the simplest story or testimony we learn to tell can ignite a fire in our souls that continues to burn as we learn to share Christ in deeper and wider ways in our new language.

> I have a superior opportunity when I am able teach the word of God in my new language, and a superior need to engage people at a heart level. (Jenny, third-year learner)

Some see "superior" only as an ACTFL language level. I tend to agree with Jenny, that it's an opportunity and a need right in front of us, calling our names. Sometimes we just need to take the labels off our language levels and put them into the vision God has given us as we dive deep and wide into the ministry to which God has called us.

Chapter Summary

- Avoiding barriers and implementing practices to go deeper and wider in our life-long pursuit of gospel fluency in our new language.

Reflect and Respond

1. Consider my international partner: How would you describe him as a life-long learner?

2. Consider the concentric circles: How do they make you more aware of the need for "breadth" and "depth" of gospel fluency in your new context?

_____

_____

3. Which of the top-ten language barriers stand out to you as particularly harmful? Explain.

_____

_____

_____

4. Which of the top-ten learning zone practices stand out to you as particularly helpful? Explain.

_____

_____

_____

My Next Faithful Step

Describe one way you resolve to put what you have learned from Chapter 8 *Deep and Wide* into practice.

_____

_____

_____

For more resources about going deeper and wider in language go to www.language180.com or scan the QR code found at the introduction and conclusion of the book.

9

Language 180

Goal: Practice *Language 180* for fruitful ongoing learning and in-language ministry.

God prepares our minds and hearts for each gospel encounter with our neighbors.

Several months into our language experience in our new city we moved into a duplex with the local community mosque compound on one side and the community football pitch on the other. We began to meet our neighbors and soon our lives were full of invitations from tea with the women to football matches with the men.

Every day, conversations flowed from one topic to the next, and I did my best to communicate the gospel whenever I could. It was about that time that I began to have my quiet time in my new language, and I shared this with my language partner, Yohannes.

Yohannes, a new believer, began doing something with me which changed the course of my life. He heard me try to share the gospel and saw that I needed a lot of help. So, he told me to share with him whatever I had been reading from God's word that morning during my quiet time.

I truly believe God brought Yohannes into my life for this purpose. I would very simply re-tell whatever I had read that morning, in my own words. Yohannes would patiently listen to me. Then he would ask a question. Maybe another. Or offer a thought. The more we did this, the richer our discussions became. We went through many Bible passages and talked about many things that helped me better understand how Yohannes, and therefore how my neighbors, heard the gospel. You see, Yohannes was not only my language partner, he was also my neighbor, and theirs.

As I prepared and practiced working through the gospel by myself, and then with Yohannes, I found myself, in my mind and heart, more ready, confident, and eager to share the gospel in my new language with my lost neighbors.

I would return home and sit with the guys at the mosque after prayers, or on the soccer pitch after practice. We would talk and through our conversation I would share Christ with them, every day, more and more, from God's word. I was becoming fluent in the gospel in the language of my neighbors. And God was using Yohannes in this process.

> *Language 180: Toward a sustained lifestyle of evangelism and discipleship in the language, we practice learning the language to communicate the gospel 3 hours per day, 60 minutes in each of three activities, for a total of 180 minutes.*

I have experienced the desperation of not feeling fluent enough to clearly and persuasively share Christ with my lost neighbors. Often distracted by grueling seasons of travel, meetings, other work, or for some other reason or excuse, I just needed to re-engage. Distractions abound in our hectic lives. I needed something to keep me alive in the language and ministry God had called me to. And I wasn't alone.

I talked with some other guys who were feeling the same way. We challenged each other to read the Bible and pray in the language for our personal devotional time. For many of us, this was an uphill climb, but well worth it and deeply enriching to our souls.

We practiced going through what we learned from God's word, every day, first by ourselves alone with God, then with a trusted friend, and then again with a lost neighbor. Our aim was to log three hours per day, one hour in each activity, for a total of 180 minutes per day. We started calling this *Language 180*.

As a solid basic-conversational-fluency-and-beyond strategy designed to get us on the path toward discourse fluency, *Language 180* raises my level of communication ability and gives me the language I need to regularly and confidently proclaim the gospel and disciple believers.

In hour one, I work through simple familiar gospel passages from *daily readings* in my new language, as a part of my personal time with God in the Bible and in prayer.

In hour two, I practice teaching the gospel from these passages with a trusted friend, neighbor, ministry partner, language partner, or teammate. We disciple one another and model what it means to evangelize our lost neighbors.

In hour three, very likely broken down into the accumulation of many conversations in the chai house, on the soccer pitch, in homes, at work, and with all fluency, I get to share the gospel with my neighbors, that very gospel message I have been preparing and practicing throughout the day. This is *Language 180*. This is *gospel fluency*.

> *Go alongside someone, a national brother or sister, helping them in tough training or discipleship situations. Bear through the embarrassment. Their response will be one of*

honor and encouragement. And they, the nationals, will do likewise. (Carlton Vandagriff)

I love to hear Yuri talk about the gospel. I try to get as much time with him as I can. He appreciates my efforts when I come prepared to teach the gospel from God's word in his language, my new language. He's a willing and patient partner in this process.

Yuri shares with me what God has said to him through his word. And I try to do the same with him. This practice has been good for both of us. I get to listen to how Yuri shares his faith, what he says, how he listens, and how he responds. This is great practice for me. But it's far more than practice. It's discipleship. It's an act of brotherly love and encouragement. We sharpen each other.

We meet as often as we can. I consider my personal time with Yuri a gift. I know I am learning so much. But I also know Yuri is growing as a disciple through our relationship and through the time we have together. We have both grown in our faith, and in our faithfulness to preach the gospel.

Yuri now regularly shares his faith with his lost neighbors from a fresh and daily understanding of the gospel in his life. This is because he spends time, as he describes it, bowing before the Lord, in God's word, and in prayer. I love that image. And he doesn't get up until he hears the gospel, once again, loud and clear; as the Lord calls him, once again, to share the gospel with his lost neighbors.

This is a great practice of discipleship and evangelism. If I can learn this from Yuri, and if I can in any way encourage Yuri in this practice, then this is how I want to spend my life.

This is how I want to spend my life!

I simply want to remind us of the importance of filling our hearts and minds with the word of God. What God does in us he will do through us. Everything emerges from our personal relationship with Jesus. We need to be in God's word and sharing his word with those around us. *Language 180* gives me the drive to share my faith and disciple people as I become more fluent in the gospel in my new language. It represents the heart and soul of *gospel fluency* as an on-going fruitful practice in cross-cultural ministry.

My neighbor Levent drank too much and beat his wife. We actually lived close enough to hear them fight and see a lot of the fallout from this on a daily basis. One evening over tea in our home with him and his wife Berrin, I asked Levent about his past. He had grown to hate his job as a government employee and so retired early. He was tired of the corruption, and wanted to start over, but he still just wasn't able to shake off some of his bad habits.

I had been reading through the book of Mark. That week I had read the story of Jesus calling Matthew out of a life of sin and corruption, and how this had changed his life. Jesus said, "It is not those who are well who need a doctor, but those who are sick. I didn't come to call the righteous, but sinners" (Mark 2:17). I thought about how God had rescued me from my life of sin and had so supernaturally changed my life.

I shared the gospel from this Bible passage and encouraged Levent and Berrin to consider Jesus' offer of new life. Levent listened hard. We prayed together. I asked God to convict them of sin, free them from addiction and abuse, and save them through faith in Christ. I sensed new hope and an open door to the gospel where there had been none. I live for these kinds of gospel conversations with my neighbors.

Daily Readings

Think about language learning as a part of your worship to the Lord. God can meet you in your second language. God can speak to you from his word in your second language. (Josiah Daniels)

I choose short vibrant readings from the Bible to guide my daily preparation, practice, and proclamation of the gospel. The gospel of Jesus Christ which I read in the Bible every day is what I practice with my language partner and with those whom I am discipling.

This is what I read, pray through, think on, and talk about with people. It's on my mind and heart. This is how the gospel enters into conversations I have with neighbors throughout the day.

I began doing *Language 180* as a daily practice working through the book of Mark. I then read through several other books, including some selected scriptures. Here are two of the reading plans I have followed. These are just examples. I encourage you to use whatever God puts on your heart. Just proclaim the gospel to yourselves and to your neighbors, every day.

MARK

WEEK	DAY 1	DAY 2	DAY 3	DAY 4	DAY 5
1	MARK 1:1-11	MARK 1:12-20	MARK 1:21-28	MARK 1:29-39	MARK 1:40-45
2	MARK 2:1-12	MARK 2:13-17	MARK 2:18-22	MARK 2:23-27	MARK 3:1-6
3	MARK 3:7-19	MARK 3:20-30	MARK 3:21-4:20	MARK 4:21-34	MARK 4:35-41
4	MARK 5:1-20	MARK 5:21-43	MARK 6:1-6	MARK 6:7-13	MARK 6:14-29
5	MARK 6:30-44	MARK 6:45-56	MARK 7:1-23	MARK 7:24-30	MARK 7:31-37
6	MARK 8:1-13	MARK 8:14-21	MARK 8:22-30	MARK 8:31-9:1	MARK 9:2-13
7	MARK 9:14-32	MARK 9:33-50	MARK 10:1-16	MARK 10:17-31	MARK 10:32-45
8	MARK 10:45-52	MARK 11:1-11	MARK 11:12-26	MARK 12:1-12	MARK 12:13-17
9	MARK 12:18-27	MARK 12:28-34	MARK 12:35-40	MARK 12:41-44	MARK 13:1-14
10	MARK 13:15-31	MARK 13:32-37	MARK 14:1-11	MARK 14:12-26	MARK 14:27-31
11	MARK 14:32-42	MARK 14:43-52	MARK 14:53-65	MARK 15:1-15	MARK 15:15-20
12	MARK 15:16-32	MARK 15:33-41	MARK 15:42-47	MARK 16:1-8	MARK 16:9-20

SELECTED TEXTS

WEEK	DAY 1	DAY 2	DAY 3	DAY 4	DAY 5
1	GEN. 1:1-2:2	PSALM 148	GEN. 2:2-25	PSALM 8	GEN. 3
2	ROM. 3:9-20	GEN. 6-9	GEN. 11:1-8	ROM. 3:21-26	ROM. 5:12-21
3	GEN. 12:1-9	ROM. 4:1-12	ROM. 4:13-25	GEN. 15:1-21	GEN. 22:1-18
4	IS. 52:13-53:12	JOHN 1:1-9	ACTS 8:26-40	GAL. 3:6-18	HEB. 11:1-19
5	EX. 31:18-32:14	EX. 32:15-33:6	EX. 33:7-23	EX. 34:1-14	LUKE 18:18-27
6	MATT. 5:1-10	MARK 5:17-24	MATT. 5:27-30	MATT. 5:38-48	ROM. 10:5-15
7	JOHN 1:10-18	JOHN 1:19-28	JOHN 1:29-34	JOHN 3:1-21	JOHN 4:1-26
8	JOHN 11:1-44	LUKE 15:11-32	LUKE 19:1-9	MATT. 27:32-56	LUKE 23:26-43
9	LUKE 23:44-55	LUKE 24:1-12	LUKE 24:36-49	ACTS 2:1-21	ACTS 2:22-47

The Gospel Diagram

Our goal is biblical fluency.

Brett had been sharing the gospel with Mahmut, but some things were still a little unclear. Brett then called Brock who came and spent an hour or so sharing a simple *Gospel Diagram* from selected Scriptures with Mahmut. This clarified the gospel for Mahmut and he placed his faith in Christ.

Brock's *Gospel Diagram* comes from years of experience evangelizing his neighbors and teaching the Bible to new believers in their language from many texts throughout Scripture – stories, prophecies and other key passages – to provide a grand narrative of Biblical truth using the following diagram.

I love how Brock keeps it simple. I annotate Brock's description using Scripture texts that he often uses, while keeping the graph itself Scripture-free. In doing so, I want us to consider how we could abundantly and effectively apply various Scripture passages using this diagram or something like it to help us learn to proclaim the whole counsel of God in our new language (Acts 20:27) while practicing *Language 180*. Brock begins with two horizontal lines that stretch to infinity.

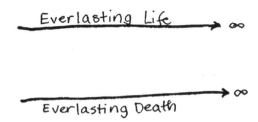

These are our only two options from now until eternity – everlasting life, or everlasting death. There are no other options. And we need to understand what they mean. We were created for eternal life with God, illustrated by the top line. The Bible explains it this way.

In the beginning, there was eternal God (Genesis 1:1-3). God created everything (1:1-26). God created man in his own image (1:27) for one purpose: to inherit everlasting life with God (1:27).

Everything was good (Genesis 1:31). God created woman to be with man and they lived perfectly in God's garden with neither shame nor sin (2:25), though God warned them not to sin (2:15-17).

Then the man and woman sinned (Genesis 3:1-7) and immediately sin and shame entered the world and came into their hearts. They were cast out of the garden. Their destination now was eternal death (illustrated by the downward "Fall" arrow.) This, too, is our destiny because of our sin. We lost everything, and fell to eternal death, forever.

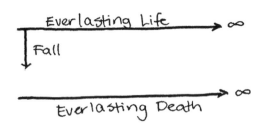

The man and woman tried to solve their shame by covering themselves with leaves (Genesis 3:7), but God provided the skin of an animal (3:21) to cover their shame. Though their relationship with God was now broken (3:23-4), God promised a descendant who would come as a savior (3:15).

Men continued to sin. Brother killed brother. All hated God. God destroyed the world with a flood. Because of his faith, God saved only Noah and his family in the ark (Genesis 6-9). Men at Babel then tried to build a tower to reach the heavens, and to make a name for themselves (Genesis 11:1-8), illustrated by the "Babel" tower image and upward arrows leading to futility. It is only through our faith in Christ – not through religion, philosophy, or good works – that we can be reconciled to God.

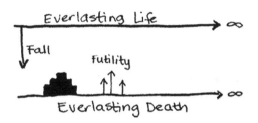

2000 years before Christ, God called Abraham out of his home to go to a land that he would show him. Abraham believed God and followed him (Genesis 12:1-3). God blessed Abraham with a son in his old age. Then God told Abraham to sacrifice his son, Isaac (22:1-14). Abraham obeyed God, and because of Abraham's wholehearted faith, God provided a ram for Abraham to sacrifice in place of his son. By faith, Abraham pointed to Jesus, God's only son, who would be sacrificed for our sins (illustrated by the "Prophecy" arrows pointing to our future hope in Christ.)

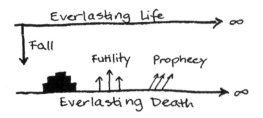

Moses (1400 BC) led the descendants of Abraham out of slavery in Egypt by the power of God through signs and wonders. The last sign was the death of each firstborn in all of Egypt. The angel of death 'passed over' the homes of the people of God, who had marked their doors with lamb's blood (Exodus 12:1-14, 21-32), and were therefore saved. By faith, Moses also pointed to Jesus (see "Prophecy" arrows) who saves us by his blood.

Isaiah (700 BC) prophesied about the eternal Lamb of God who takes away our sins (Isaiah 52:13 – 53:12) pointing to Christ's sacrificial death. John 1:1-18 says that Jesus Christ was the Word of God, God himself who had come to live among us. John the Baptist said of Jesus Christ who came to earth as a baby and died on the cross for our sins, "Behold the Lamb of God who takes away the sin of the world!" (John 1:29) illustrated by the cross of Christ. Jesus died on the cross to take away our sins. Only when we put our faith in Jesus can we be cleansed from sin, reconciled to God, and inherit eternal life.

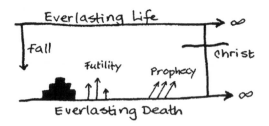

Jesus testified of himself as the fulfillment of all law and prophecy (Matthew 5:17). He prophesied of his death and resurrection (Luke 18:31-33), and actually died on the cross for our sins, and rose again from the grave (Luke 23-24). Jesus is God's only son (John 3:16), and those who believe in him are saved from eternal death to inherit eternal life (John 20:24-31).

We have all sinned and fall short of God's glory (Romans 3:23). But, God showed his love for us in that while we were sinners Christ died for us (Romans 5:8). We deserve eternal death, but God's gift to us is eternal life through faith in Christ Jesus our Lord (Romans 6:23).

Jesus is the Passover Lamb (1 Cor 5:7), the last and only sacrifice (Hebrews 10:12), the final word of God to us, the heir of all things, through whom all things were created, the radiance of God's glory, the exact imprint of his nature, who upholds the universe by the word of his power, who made purification for our sins by his death on the cross, and is now seated at the right hand of the Majesty on high (Hebrews 1:1-3). "For you are saved by grace through faith, and this is not from yourselves; it is God's gift – not from works, so that no one can boast (Ephesians 2:8-9).

This is the faith that transforms our lives. This is the gospel message we are called to know, live, preach, and teach. As we follow Christ's commission to make disciples of all peoples let us never pursue anything less than a full-on commitment toward total fluency in our gospel message, encompassing the entire breadth and depth of all biblical truth in the languages and cultures God calls us to learn.

> *We cannot transmit the faith we do not know.*
> *(Jen Wilkin, from The Future of Missions)*

Chapter Summary

- Dedicating three hours per day to *Language 180*: Personal preparation, focused practice, and fluent proclamation.
- A look at daily scripture readings and the Gospel Diagram as ways to apply *Language 180*.

Reflect and Respond

1. How do you study or envision studying the Bible and praying in your new language? (E.g., Do you read a short passage, write in your journal, or take audio notes? Be specific.)

   _____

   _____

   _____

2. Describe how you would engage key people in your life – language partners, ministry partners, neighbors – to help you improve your ability to teach the Bible as you practice what you've prepared. Take a moment to pray for these people, even if you don't know them yet.

   _____

   _____

   _____

3. Consider to this statement: *When we intentionally prepare and practice "gospel fluency" each day, we are prompted to share the gospel with our lost neighbors each day.* Imagine Language 180 (or something like it) as a daily practice. Describe the challenges; the benefits.

_____

_____

_____

My Next Faithful Step

Describe one way you resolve to put what you have learned from Chapter 9 *Language 180* into practice.

_____

_____

_____

To learn more about how to put "Language 180" into practice go to www.language180.com or scan the QR code found at the introduction and conclusion of the book.

10

1000 Cups of Tea

Goal: Converse the gospel in
your new language.

Recovering the lost art of
neighboring across
cultures.

My pastor Mike and I would meet for coffee every week
when we were in the US for a season. It was a highlight. I just
enjoyed the time together. We talked about a lot of things.
Common interests. What happened over the past week, joys,
needs; always food for my soul. "How are the kids?...How was
your week?...How's work?...Did you guys have a good time at
the picnic last Thursday?...How's was your wife's visit with

her sister?" Whatever we talked about just added great mortar to our friendship.

I don't remember a lot of the specifics we talked about. I *do* remember the care, the friendship, the love; that I mattered to Mike; that he was my pastor and friend, and that our time together was important to him. It was time together that I loved. And I think what I loved most about this time was that it was never rushed, and somehow the conversation would wind its way into our hearts. Mike would share what was going on in his life, and ask me how I was doing, at a heart level.

We had long finished our coffee, and Mike just knew when and how to drill down, inviting me to explore our hearts together. Those were some of my best times with my pastor. Encouraging, God-honoring, sometimes a little messy, but I always came away from those times spiritually uplifted. "People may not remember what I preach, but they remember how I pastor" (Mike Fritcher).

I realized there is a certain understanding, in a *discourse* sense – if we were to call this kind of conversation "discourse" – and even in a *spiritual* sense – if we were to pull back the curtain to see the inner workings of the Spirit of God throughout the conversation – to how topics of conversation and discussion tend to oscillate from more surface levels of mutual interest, to deeper levels of heart interest. Mike knew how to do this. He was wise. He was discerning. He was a pastor. He did this with such authenticity, such genuine affection and care. I felt loved and trusted. I felt pastored.

I think of the many times Jesus dined with sinners, tax collectors, his disciples, Pharisees, good friends such as Mary, Martha, and Lazarus. He must have spent hours and hours with people in their homes, "reclining at the table" (Luke 11:37, Mark 2:15, John 12:2, etc.). These verses do far more than just create context and setting. They demonstrate the abundance of time and attention Jesus must have intentionally invested with people to reach them where they were, as he ministered to them. It was through hours and hours with neighbors in their homes, over meals, just being together, that we see the path to the gospel Jesus trod with them.

It was through hours and hours with neighbors in their homes, over meals, just being together, that we see the path to the gospel Jesus trod with them.

In Luke 19, when Jesus first met Zacchaeus, he told him to climb down from the tree because he was going with him to his home to be his guest. Zacchaeus came down and welcomed him gladly. Jesus honored Zacchaeus by entering his home, at risk of his reputation. Zacchaeus was the chief tax collector, and people grumbled that Jesus went to dine with him in his home.

Something happened to Zacchaeus' heart during this encounter that brought him to repentance. We can infer that Jesus honored Zacchaeus by entering his home, and probably showed him great affection as a good doctor would his sick patient. Whatever they talked about at the dinner table must have led to a level of trust and openness that brought Zacchaeus' heart to a steeping point of hearing and receiving the gospel Jesus taught him.

In John 21, the disciples had been fishing all night and had caught nothing. Jesus told them where to cast their net and in one attempt they caught 153 fish. Peter dragged the net ashore and John, the writer, emphasizes that even with that many fish, the net was not torn. Jesus invited them to breakfast. These fishermen must have had a lot to talk about as they ate. The Bible then says that, "when they had finished breakfast, Jesus said to Simon Peter, 'Simon, son of John, do you love me more than these?'" (John 21:15).

116

I don't want to miss the effect of this transition. It does not say that Jesus asked Simon Peter this question *during* breakfast, rather very specifically tells us that he asked him when they *had finished eating*. There is something very special and powerful about their dining together, on the beach, right then at that time, that communicated mutual affection, trust, and created an environment of grace. Jesus knew the rhythm, and John, Peter, and the others got it. They had just dined together. They knew Jesus loved them. This was an incredibly important part of the whole dynamic of Jesus reinstating Peter. He didn't bark the order. We need to remember that when Jesus pulled Peter aside to talk with him, his fingers were probably still greasy from the fish they shared together, and his clothes smelled like the smoke of the fire they were sitting around.

> The single desire of our hearts can be expressed in a thousand ways, through the loss, beliefs, pain, shame, hope, dreams, failures, and fears through a thousand scripts of life, over a thousand cups of tea.

I live in a tea culture. There is a certain art to brewing tea correctly. It has to steep. You have to know how to boil the water, when to add the leaves, and how long you need to wait until it's ready to serve. I remember hearing a colleague laugh about the first time he was called upon to serve tea. It turned out to be hot water and leaves – tasteless! His guests applauded his efforts, and then proceeded to show him how to really make tea.

Conversations, like tea, need to steep. They take time with people face to face. Our hearts are warmed by the friendship, the honor, the affection. Sometimes we just need to watch and learn from our neighbors how to do this.

Let's Drink More Unscheduled Tea!

My German friend Marcus told me about a conversation he recently had in his new language here in this city with two local friends who were both followers of Christ. One of them asked, "Why are we Christians so anti-social?" He said it shocked and confused him, so he asked him what he meant by that.

Marcus' local friends described recently attending a neighborhood meeting at their former place of worship, and then getting calls from at least five people the next week, just asking to hang out, have tea, or go to a movie – no other agenda. Anyone who did not show up got called. "Hey, what's wrong? Why aren't you here? Are you okay?" And this happened all the time, every week. They always called each other up, and they always went out for tea.

At first, Marcus protested, "It's unbiblical to not love each other." But after hearing several more examples of the same kind of experience, he began to wonder, "Do you think this is because local Christians have learned how to socialize with each other from us foreigners?"

Marcus explained to them that we in the West often feel that to call and invite someone right away seems like pressuring someone. To call every two or three days is against our Western culture. To invite someone without a reason seems awkward for us. To just knock at the door and visit someone without planning it a week in advance feels rude.

Sadly, Marcus' local friends understood all too well what he meant. One of them confessed that when his American believing friend recently invited him for a meal, he sensed an agenda. Sure enough, he had one. Yes, he sighed, he is now well adjusted to the way Christian foreigners behave. When Marcus asked him if he would just show up at a Christian friend's doorstep uninvited, he said no – but he does it all the time with his local non-believing friends.

I was convicted when I heard this story from Marcus. Together we agreed to make a habit of calling for no other reason than to ask friends and neighbors how they are. "Let's show them that we care, that we think about them, that time with them is important just because we are with them. Let's drink more unscheduled tea!"

I shared this story with Mateo, a Latino friend living in our city. Mateo has led many people to Christ. He spends lots of time with people. He disciples people. I treasure his advice.

"Let's do less meetings and drink more tea together. What we do in our culture is not important, if people here think different. The way local people do things must be more effective, in order to achieve God's Kingdom purpose here. Love needs to be lived in a practical way."

Considering our value for community, we need to put this into practice in our lifestyle with our neighbors. If our neighbors practice community with each other better than we do with each other, let alone with them, then we are not practicing who we say we are. We are a community of faith. We are also a faith of community.

Tom Brewster described a conversation over tea in his home with an African neighbor who confessed how so often he was received by foreign believers at the door post of their homes as if to say (as often they did), "What do you want?"

About two and a half hours into the conversation it became apparent why Tom's guest had come when he reached into his jacket and pulled out a gift wrapped in newspaper. Do we ever wonder, as Tom did, "How many gifts have never been given?"[28]

How many times have we found ourselves just trying to get something done with a neighbor, a disciple, or a national co-worker, without inviting them into our lives for conversation and tea? "Some things just can't be done leaning against a door post."[29]

> *Some things just can't be done leaning against a door post. (Tom Brewster)*

What does it mean for us to honor our neighbors enough to give ourselves to the time and space needed to have tea together, regularly, with no agenda? We must love the person in front of us enough to put down our phones and attend to them.

When we come into our conversations and relationships with an agenda, people sense it and will not robotically respond to what we're driving at. We don't drive people to the cross, we lead them.

> *We don't drive people to the cross, we lead them.*

It's often through hours and hours of "steeping" our relationships and conversations in genuine affection and trust that leads people to the gospel, to respond in repentance and faith, as Peter did, and Zacchaeus, and so many others. This is essentially what it means to converse the gospel.

Conversing the Gospel

The Essential Dialogue

One of the special advantages we have as guests and as language and culture learners is the opportunity to come into conversations, often over tea or coffee, with a certain amount of preparation allowing us to dialogue on topics of mutual interest as we learn, understand, and begin to share the gospel in meaningful ways. In other words, we need to learn to converse the gospel, where our speaking and listening weave into the essential dialogue and discussion in natural and compelling ways.

120

I spoke with a learner who had done some research on his neighbor's home village in central Anatolia before meeting with him for tea one day. The preparation he had done provided great context for their conversation. My friend's neighbor was so honored that my friend showed such a genuine interest in his village. This led to multiple future conversations about childhood, family, and the differences between life there and life in the city, and even opened up an invitation to the village, to meet his neighbor's relatives and neighbors. Every conversation brought new opportunities to learn and prepare a little bit more for the next conversation through thoughtful questions and discussions on related topics.

One of the things we try to help learners practice is the art of transitioning from one topic to another. When we engage in conversations with our neighbors, we commonly enter these conversations unprepared and, therefore, to some extent, unengaged. As much as possible, let us aspire to enter into conversations in their language with this mindset: "I am interested in being here with you. I want to engage in topics of common interest. I have been thinking about this. You are important to me."

This means we need to take extra time and energy to engage our neighbors on topics they think about and things they experience, perhaps even preparing some thoughts to share or questions to ask. We learn to share the gospel in the flow of normal conversation. We listen, respond, and engage. We need to learn to prepare the tea and serve it well, with the true humility of genuine love and sympathetic interest.

When we get to do this, when we learn to humbly and genuinely honor our neighbors in ways that speak to their hearts, we begin to see the joy of the Lord percolating through the conversation, working as leaven through the relationship. This can make all the difference toward sharing the gospel when we learn to practice this well.

Breadcrumbs

Conversations are never memorized.

One of my neighbors recently compared conversations we often have in our language to that of following breadcrumbs on a trail. (I was actually surprised when he asked if I knew the story of *Hansel and Gretel*.) We never map out entire conversations in our heads as we enter into them. If so, then they are not really conversations. Rather, we get to pursue them with wonder and interest as one conversational morsel leads to another.

I was talking with Ron and Amy about gospel conversations during their recent visit to our city from their place of ministry. I mentioned what my neighbor had said about breadcrumbs. Ron later shared this beautiful testimony.

> As I was thinking more about the breadcrumbs idea and just how relational people are in our part of the world, I thought about a dinner we recently had with our neighbors. We were there for several hours, and conversation was mostly small talk or random things, bits of truth shared that fit the moment, but not big chunks. Then around midnight the guys asked me to compare Christianity and their religion. It was a super sweet conversation. But I don't think I would have been heard if it didn't slowly lead to that point where they wanted to know.
>
> About a month later, the brother-in-law from that family grabbed me as we left their house and said, "I want to know more about these things. I'll invite you to my house soon where I'm not a guest, too. We can speak freely." He invited us to come when we get back. Praying it happens.

I love hearing about gospel moments like these. I pray along with Ron that more of these will happen, like the conversation he anticipates with his neighbor's brother-in-law. It is conversations *just like these* that God is inviting us into with our neighbors.

> I also thought about Sam and his questions as we've studied gospel truth. They seem random sometimes, but they're not random to him. He asked me one day as we were studying how we can be saved, "Do you shave your armpits?" I was super confused but answered. And for once, I asked why. He said, "In my religion if I don't trim or shave every 40 days, then I will be unholy and unclean. In Christianity do you have this rule? Or are you really saved by someone else's actions?" Breadcrumbs... (Ron, co-worker).

What an interesting conversation…and, how beautiful for Ron to tune-in and respond to what Sam was really saying and seeking! We may wonder in amazement how through seemingly random "breadcrumb" conversations like these we actually get to meet our neighbors right where they are. And that as we understand and share thoughts, beliefs, desires, concerns, and hopes, we get to introduce them to Christ in incredibly meaningful ways. But are we willing to invest the time, listen well, attend to the relationships, and pursue these essential conversations for the sake of the gospel among them?

Midnight Football

I recently played a midnight (soccer) football match with some believing friends and a group of guys who I later discovered hail from what some refer to as the "mixed-martial-arts capital of the world." I had no idea what I was getting into! A few of us foreigners were the weak links on the teams, so I just followed Jack's advice to "run fast and try to stay out of the way." It felt great to be alive after the match!

The next evening, we had tea with one of their leaders. Ali is well respected in his community, as well as in his village, hundreds of miles away. He talked about his childhood and the languages and cultures found deep in the mountains of his mysterious homeland. Ali asked my colleagues to join him on a trip home, quite a unique invitation to this part of the country, and one that came from someone with enough social capital to actual back it up. I am convinced the hours spent playing football and having tea with Ali and his friends are what built the trust required to extend this kind of an offer to enter the homeland of some of the most unengaged and unreached people on earth.

As we sat and drank tea with Ali, I thought about how much these friends of mine have lovingly given up for a greater gain. Some things were obvious – moving their families, setting up business, developing ministry partners. But it's probably more often in the unsuspecting ways – getting laughed at when we speak funny, kicking a ball around in the middle of the night (when we'd rather be at home with our families, or in bed), and just getting time with these guys on their turf; playing their games, and speaking their language, made all the difference. This is the stuff of life that seems to lead to invitations into homes, and to the gospel in conversations.

Kofta

Not long ago I went with my college-age son to get some kofta at a new buffet in our neighborhood. It was pouring rain as our kofta friend welcomed us, his only customers, into his tiny place. We sat on barstools, drinking the tea he offered, with only the counter separating us from his workstation. As he kneaded the ingredients, Adam asked (as he always does) where he was from. He told us stories of the Black Sea where he had worked as a chef, offering specific and downright fascinating details about breakfast preparation in various locations.

More interesting to me though was watching my son honor this big brother throughout our conversation. That's how Adam viewed him. Through his mannerisms and responses, sharing about what he was studying in school and his future plans, Adam showed true interest and respect as our new friend offered advice on life, work, honesty, and obedience.

When the wraps were done, I gave our kofta friend a 20 in the local currency, more than enough for our food, and waited for change as other customers arrived. He suddenly hesitated – a simple miscalculation, but he wrote it down again just to make sure. Adam caught the glimmer of shame because of our friend's poor math skills and responded immediately, "Thank you, big brother. You just instructed me in honesty, and now you have shown me by example."

Virtues of the Christian life are more often caught, viewed, and demonstrated, than they are taught, and this can happen in such unsuspecting moments. Our unexpected exchange as we left the shop seemed trivial, but it really was a big deal, once I opened my eyes. And it has opened the door to many future conversations over tea, kofta, honor, the topic of honesty, and the gospel. (I try to go when it rains.)

I don't think it ever crossed Adam's mind not to respect this poor man's honorable work, and the good food he prepared for us, as his big brother. I asked Adam about this as we walked home. "Simple," he said, "honesty is a far more important life virtue than math skills." I agreed. I thought of a question a neighbor once asked a colleague, "Do you love me because you want me to become a Christian, or do you want me to become a Christian because you love me?"

We may need to ask ourselves this as we consider how and why we spend time with our neighbors, and as we share the gospel with them; toward loving them, honoring them, and considering the integrity of our intentions as we share Christ with them. We love our neighbors out of our obedience to God, and because God loves us, and this is why and how we demonstrate God's love to them. We know God's love because we are redeemed, and the love of God constrains us as we live out our lives before our neighbors in our new communities.

The invitation to the gospel is supremely enriched by our genuine expressions of love. This may indeed happen over a single brief encounter, where we may never see each other again, but it more often happens in those regular, repeated, and unhurried, "steeping" encounters that happen over the span of a thousand cups of tea.

Chapter Summary

- Learning to converse the gospel as we invest time (or drink "unscheduled tea") with our precious neighbors.

Reflect and Respond

1. Who do you spend time with every day? How do you plan to reach out to your lost neighbors? (This can be challenging in many urban contexts.)

   _____

   _____

2. When you spend time with your neighbors, what do you talk about? What are their common interests, deeper concerns? How do you relate to them?

   _____

   _____

3. Consider this statement: *Conversations, like tea, need to steep. They take time, with people, face to face. Our hearts are warmed by the friendship, the honor, the affection. We need to watch and learn how to do this from our neighbors.* Share a way you could honor your neighbors by spending time with them without an agenda (e.g., unscheduled tea).

_____

_____

_____

4. Consider this statement: *We need to learn to converse the gospel, where our speaking and listening weave into the essential dialogue and discussion.* Share how you envision learning to "converse the gospel" in your new language.

_____

_____

_____

My Next Faithful Step

Describe one way you resolve to put what you have learned from Chapter 10 *1000 Cups of Tea* into practice.

_____

_____

_____

For more resources on practicing "1000 Cups of Tea" go to www.language180.com or scan the QR code found at the introduction and conclusion of the book.

11

God Speaks My Language

Goal: Share your testimony;
pray for your neighbors.

The power of ~~testimony~~

Six months after arriving to our new city we had reached a breaking point. As with most journeys, it started out with a lot of enthusiasm. We began learning language and getting to know our neighbors. We almost immediately faced unexpected personal challenges. Pregnant with our first child, Jenn was regularly harassed by men, even afraid at times to leave the protection of our home. Our front door then became the neighborhood garbage dump. With a growing sewage pile-up and a rat infestation we felt more and more unwelcomed. Complications in the birth of our son left us hanging by a thread, uncertain about our future. Hurting and confused, we desperately needed God's comfort.

As we cried out to our Heavenly Father, he indeed met with us and comforted us. God's comfort and presence, more than anything else that first year, was the message of the gospel to us as a young family. From that overflow, this became our testimony of the gospel to our neighbors.

We learned to pray from Psalm 61, what it meant to lift our hearts up to God, "Hear my cry, O God, listen to my prayer, from the end of the earth I call out to you." We sensed God's hand lifting us out of the pit (Psalm 40) as we waited on him. Praying through Psalm 23, we sensed God's presence with us even as we went through this dark valley. We found God's deep compassion for us as he spoke tenderly from Isaiah 40, "Comfort, comfort my people." And as the chapter concludes, we too began to learn what it means to wait on the Lord, to put our hope in the Lord, for he would renew our strength.

> Now may the God of hope fill you with all joy and peace as you believe [for the impossible, for the unseen, for his supernatural intervention, those things that are yet to be] so that you may overflow with [be overwhelmed by and abound in] HOPE by the power of the Holy Spirit (Romans 15:13).

Jenn asked me to include our parenthetical notes (and the capital letters) along with this scripture (above) because that's how we remember it spilling out in our prayers and journals.

It was during times like these we were deeply comforted by Paul's open-hearted testimony throughout 2 Corinthians. He introduces his letter with these amazing words of comfort and hope in the midst of severe difficulties and suffering. In just the first paragraph (1:3-7), Paul uses the word "comfort" an astounding nine times. Count them.

Parakaleo ("comfort") literally means "to call alongside," abiding comfort, resident comfort. God knows our affliction, and his compassion and mercy toward us are deeply personal as he comes alongside us with his abiding presence. He is our hope and strength. And as we experience once again the incredible joy and hope of life in Christ, we come into a deeper understanding of what it means to host Christ's presence in our lives, and we regain the joy of stewarding the gospel as our supreme identity in Christ.

We need the gospel as much as those we are teaching. (Richard)

The reason I share this story is because chances are it's your story, too. Anyone who has lived in a totally new culture and learned a new language has some sort of identification with what I just shared. The details may look a little different, but each one of us has gone through, or is going through experiences where we come to the end of ourselves, and in desperation we cry out to our God who saves.

And that's the point. Our story is that Jesus saves us. This is good news. And this is the good news that we tell others who desperately need to hear it.

Jesus calls us to the nations, but he first calls us to himself. Just as we received the gospel when we first came to Christ, the gospel comes alive again right before our eyes as we receive God's goodness, his comfort, his salvation in our times of need. We live full circle. Ours is a living witness to the good news of Jesus Christ. Our supreme task – our delight – is to remind ourselves of the gospel each day. As we speak the gospel to our hearts, then in the overflow we speak it from our hearts. This is the daily testimony – our testimony – that we bear to our lost neighbors.

Back home over coffee one day with our pastor, Mike, and his wife, JonAnne, we were talking about the challenges of cross-cultural ministry. How can we be more aware of God at work in conversations and situations? How can we be more spiritually attentive to what we are hearing in those encounters? JonAnne summed it up well, "When I'm in those conversations, I really feel God speaks my language. He shows me who I am in him, and what he's given me, and how I can share it with my neighbors both here and around the world."

JonAnne spoke of finding her space in ministry and reaching out to people around her in need of the gospel. She described "hearing God speak her language" as the message of the gospel from God's word spoken to her heart through quiet moments in his presence, empowering her to sow into the lives of those around her. She talked of walking in faith and taking risks to share Christ with people. JonAnne shared with us that through this walk of faith and obedience she has been able to see God change lives.

We need to be fluent in sharing the gospel with our lost neighbors, in listening and attending to their response. But, more than anything, we need to be fluent in hearing Jesus. We need to hear him speak our language, as he reminds us of the gospel from his word and by his Spirit, as he guides us to our lost neighbors and gives us wisdom, insight, words to say, and ears to hear.

Perhaps our testimony today for our neighbor is about something God did in our lives years ago, or maybe something he showed us in his word just yesterday. It may be a simple gospel story we told our kids or our roommate last week. As our neighbors hear these stories, they may at first only indirectly relate to them, yet this may very well be the intended posture and understanding from which God woos their hearts. God delights in the word of our testimony, our personal witness of the gospel at work in our lives. "Our inner person is being renewed day by day" (2 Corinthians 4:16).

If we truly believe in the transforming work of God in our lives, then our testimony of salvation should be as fresh and vibrant today as it was yesterday, or even more! And we carry this testimony in our minds and hearts, the gospel, to hungry souls, hungry to hear these words of life.

The gospel fills our hearts, restores our souls, and transforms our minds. It defines our lives, captivates our spirits, and renews our testimonies. When we speak the gospel from God's word, it is borne from our hearts and fills the atmosphere with the presence of Jesus. We bear the aroma of Christ. We speak words of great hope. We have confidence not in ourselves, but in the message of the gospel. What does it mean for us to have a posture to really engage? It means we have a story to tell. It means we anticipate hearing something from the Lord from his word, and therefore we indeed have something to say. In other words, we anticipate that God is wanting to communicate the gospel through our testimony to our neighbors.

How does this practically work out? Whether we share our testimonies, carry tracts, write out verses and thoughts, show a short video clip, read directly from our Bible, or do all of the above, the important thing is we need to be vitally aware of the extent of our investment, in the moment, with people, as we communicate the message of the gospel and engage in their response.

As believers, we are called to communicate the gospel, and we are also compelled to understand and respond to the hunger that people have for the gospel. This is the compassion of Christ. As we share, we also meditate on the gospel, on the very words of our Lord, and God will prompt us during our conversations with people as we remain in quiet dialogue with him.

We need to start with what we have. If all we have is five minutes of time, language, or relationship, let's start with that. Five minutes in a seemingly pointless conversation can open up amazing doors to a whole community of language practice and gospel ministry. As we pray with anticipation, and as we keep our eyes and hearts open to all opportunities, we'll begin to discover that God gives us redemptive encounters with people all the time.

Tell them why it's real! Just tell people what God has done for you!
(Timur, national partner)

Not long ago I was listening to 1 John in the language while I was running. As I was listening and meditating on the Scripture, I came to the beginning of chapter 3 and suddenly remembered that these were the verses my mom shared with me when I gave my life to Christ as a child. I had read this passage many times. "Why remember this now?" I wondered. Right then I came to the corner of the road where an older lady was standing. I'd seen her before, getting on a minibus to head to work. She was alone this day and the bus was still down the road. I knew why the Spirit had prompted that memory. I had just a couple minutes before her bus came. I stopped and shared this one verse with her. "See what great love the Father has given us that we should be called God's children – and we are!" (1 John 3:1).

I told her how God had led my mother to share this verse with me, that I was God's child by his great love and mercy, through faith in Jesus, and that is the reason I wanted to share it with her that she would know God's love for her. She let me pray for her and I gave her the audio scriptures just as her bus pulled up. As she got on the bus, she smiled and put her hand to her heart in thanks. I never saw her again.

I've heard these referred to as "miracle moments." Jesus lived in the moment well. He responded to what seemed to be moments of spiritual opportunity. I think they happen all the time all around us. We're just not very aware of them. Jesus was.

In John 5, Jesus asks a lame man at a pool, "Do you want to get well?" (v. 6). We are not told specifically why he zeroed in on this man, and then asked him this question. But we do know that he did it in that moment with the intention to heal him. So right then and there, the lame man told Jesus his life story of 38 years of disappointment in about 15 seconds. Amazing. Jesus opened the door with his question, "Do you want to get well?" and the man walked right to the gospel. Jesus knew this man in a moment. How do we know our neighbors? It may take longer than a moment, but God is at work in every encounter. We live in similar moments of decision. Many of these are moments to immerse, or disconnect; to engage, or to walk on.

Prayer – The Buoyancy of the Gospel

Do we pray until our hearts break for the lost?
(Sean, co-worker)

I don't understand it, but God answers prayer. Sean spoke of God giving him a renewed burden and greater passion to share the gospel with his lost neighbors as he labored for hours and days interceding for them. That in itself is an amazing answer to prayer which inspires me to pray more! I am convinced that as we pray more for our lost neighbors, we can expect in faith that God is already at work in us, in them, and in the future gospel encounters we will have with them. Prayer really is the buoyancy of the gospel.

As we pray for our lost neighbors in our new community, God gives us insights that only come through that time we spend in prayer. As we pray, God will speak to our minds and hearts, giving us greater compassionate awareness and sensitivity to his interests in those for whom we intercede, our relationships with them, possibly even concerning the next conversation we may have with them. God will direct us in these encounters, for his glory.

Prayer gives us confidence and hope in God's purposes for our lost neighbors, strengthening our faith as we rise to engage them with the gospel. Prayer and intercession should be our daily practice, an anticipation of gospel proclamation opportunities that emerge from our daily mental and spiritual posture. We should be in constant conversation with God as we meditate on his word. "Devote yourselves to prayer; stay alert in it with thanksgiving" (Colossians 4:2).

We enter with confidence and authority through prayer into the word of God. As we intercede for our lost neighbors, we begin to anticipate God-directed gospel encounters with them. This is how we begin to live, looking for "miracle moments" with people all around us.

Do we wonder why we don't have more opportunities to share the gospel with our lost neighbors? The better question may be, do we wonder why we miss so many opportunities because we fail to pray, and therefore we aren't looking for these moments with spiritual readiness?

> Nothing demonstrates gentleness and respect quite like praying for someone else in their presence. When you don't know what else to say you can always ask the question, "Can I pray for you?", and then do it right then and there.[30]

God has a direct interest in every conversation. When we pray for people and with people even as we have conversations with them, we become more aware of God's purposes for the relationship, more aware of his activity in the relationship, and more aware of his direction in the conversation.

Some gospel conversations may even surprise us. As we pray, God may even give us supernatural wisdom for transformational encounters that may go against cultural norms. Think of Jesus sitting by a well asking a Samaritan woman for a drink or responding to a Pharisee who came to him at night. Somewhat surprising and confusing for Nicodemus, "you must be born again" was exactly the gospel message he needed to hear, right then and there.

What may appear to be counter-cultural may be exactly the message or invitation God is prompting us to extend. While we do want to be appropriate in our communication, God calls us to be transformational in the encounter.

Pray constantly!
(1 Thessalonians 5:17)

A lifestyle of prayer is one of the best ways for us to live well in the daily ministry moments God gives us, praying always, and responding immediately. How well do we spend time with people? It may be normal just to spend time with them, and complete our business, and then we're done...but what if there was more? A bigger assignment? Did we pray for that person, perhaps silently, or perhaps aloud by invitation, as we were with them? Do we pray for them by name before we meet them? Do we ask and anticipate God to enter into the conversation, a conversation that is not just about God, rather of God actively giving us insight and softening their hearts right there before our eyes as we engage them with the gospel?

Do stories our neighbors tell us, and questions they ask us, in conversations with them, influence our prayers for them? What do we really know about their lives? Their needs? Interests? Families? Maybe not much...yet. Maybe we just need more time. Or maybe we just haven't asked because we haven't thought about it or prayed about it. Many of our neighbors want to tell us stories of things going on in their lives. Will they at first be difficult to understand? Probably. Therefore, we need to all the more pray, listen, and respond as we engage them with the gospel.

Philip's miraculous encounter with the Ethiopian in the desert on the road to Gaza (Acts 8:26-39) began with simply listening and responding to the Spirit's guidance. The Bible says Philip ran to him, heard the Ethiopian reading from Isaiah 53, and then asked him, "Do you understand what you are reading?" to which he responded, "How can I unless someone guides me?" and then invited Philip to explain it.

> Then Philip opened his mouth and beginning with this scripture he told him the good news about Jesus.
> Acts 8:35 ESV

Do we pray, with anticipation, for encounters with people who need Jesus, in the sense that God delights to bring us into these miracle moments of spiritual engagement? Are we responsive? Do we live with confidence in the authority in Christ, that he is guiding us to these encounters, and in these conversations? Things may look different than we had planned that morning. They almost always do. These are teachable moments, gospel moments.

Practically, this may mean learning and regularly using words of blessing whenever we can. Jon does this in my new language every time I'm with him, with everyone. I've heard Jon say many times, "God gives us the gift of communication to bless" and he lives by this motto. He engages in conversations using whatever he knows and has learned through the people he's met. He shares what he can. And opportunities to share the gospel open up when I am with him. That's always encouraging.

Several months ago, on one of Jon's visits to our city, an elderly gentleman greeted us as we were walking through his neighborhood. As is his practice, Jon reached out with gospel words and verses of blessing using what language he could. Hamdi responded with gratitude and I missed an opportunity right then and there. That night, Hamdi was on my heart. I prayed for Hamdi. The next day Jon and I went back and by God's grace we found Hamdi in the same neighborhood and we did what I believe we were supposed to do the day before. We spent an hour sharing the gospel with Hamdi.

Excavating our Hearts

The testimony of a language learner

It's amazing how something as simple as learning to tell a story in the context of a real-life conversation in our new language can be so emotionally destabilizing. I felt like I failed the first time I tried to tell my neighbors a short gospel story in my new language. I was able to speak with confidence as I told it to my language partner but had no such confidence in speaking with my neighbors. I came away from that experience feeling pretty miserable.

The pain of failure in our language learning pursuits can be very real and pervasive. I've personally grieved for myself and for others who struggle with this. The fear of failure is a common struggle among language learners who regularly put themselves into situations like this, again and again, using new language, risking mistakes at every turn. Sometimes all we can pray is, "Lord, give me the heart to fight and lose."

I'm not that confident learner who has never felt the excruciating pain of trying hard yet failing. Sometimes we just feel spent, with nothing left in our emotional tanks but shame, fear, defeat, and humiliation. So, where do we go from there? There is really only one place to go. We go to God. We realize our complete dependence on him, give him our humiliation, and move forward one step at a time on the path of courageous humility.

This path and posture of humility in our language learning needs to be prayed, voiced, shared, received, and celebrated as we discover our second language identities the Lord forms in us, in the midst of transitions that are often excruciatingly painful. It is in death to self that we find greater hope in Christ, and we learn to embrace the noble irony of this calling. We are called to reach the end of ourselves, so that we can begin anew, depending on Christ as he introduces us to our gospel calling in a fresh way in our new language and community.

This is deeply personal, profoundly redemptive, and immensely powerful as we testify of the glory of the gospel in our lives, and through our lives, to our lost neighbors. This is the glorious paradox, that as we struggle to tell them the good news in our new language, they somehow will hear it loud and clear, not despite the testimony of our struggle, but through it, and because of it.

So, where does this leave us? It leaves us identifying with the Lord, with our lost neighbors, and with a hope and a joy that is magnified in our personal understanding, and expression, as we walk through the pain and despair of deep personal failure and into the reality of the gospel that permeates and lifts us from our very real struggles.

In reality, our gospel fluency comes alive when we proclaim it from this posture of victory in Christ, even as we struggle in our language. This is our testimony, as we share Scriptures from our minds and hearts with words that communicate the gospel in and through our lives as we engage our neighbors.

It is only by God's marvelous grace that we overcome the crushing weight and defeat of cross-cultural failure. This is an astonishing crucible of identity in which we personally engage as we discover what it means to be people of the gospel called to the nations and to our lost neighbors.

Nelli

Whenever I talked with them, all I could ever think about was "Jesus."[31]

As I consider our call to reach *gospel fluency* in our new languages, I am deeply aware how fully and wholly we must depend on God's grace and on his strength in all of this; and I am reminded of Nelli and her husband Yuri who host our house church in their home. With no use of her arms and legs, restricted to her bed and wheelchair, physically unable to do anything for herself, Nelli is fully dependent on Yuri as her caregiver. In a more real sense, she has placed her dependence, her faith, fully in God. How do I know this? Because every time I see her lying in her bed, she peppers our conversation – as she does with neighbors she encounters everyday – with Scriptures she has read through and through, meditated on, believes in, and testifies…and she exhorts me to do the same.

Recently, my youngest son and I were visiting Nelli with a few of his friends. In true form, she exhorted these boys to read Philippians 4:12-13 from God's word with these instructions:

> First, have your dad read the passage aloud, slowly, and twice through. Listen hard, listen to God.
> Then wait, in silent prayer, for five minutes, and think about what you just heard.
> Then take five minutes to write down what you just thought about.
> Then, as a group, talk about what you wrote down, one by one.

Simple, profound teaching. I was not at all surprised to hear as these boys shared – each with tears in his eyes – what the Lord had so powerfully taught them from his word through this dear sister's exhortation:

> *I am able to do all things through him who strengthens me (Philippians 4:13).*

Chapter Summary

- The power of our testimonies
- Intercessory prayer: the buoyancy of the gospel.
- Tuning in as God leads us into gospel encounters.

Reflect and Respond

1. Describe recently sharing your testimony with your lost neighbors. If nothing comes to mind, how do you envision doing this?

\
\
\

2. Do you anticipate gospel encounters with your neighbors? What is one way you can be more attentive to God's work in their lives and in your relationship with them?

\
\
\

3. *Ours is a living witness to the good news of Jesus Christ, a daily testimony that we bear to our lost neighbors.* As you reflect on this statement, describe one thing that God has done in your recent past or is doing right now in your life that you can share with your lost neighbors as a testimony of the gospel in your life.

\
\
\

4. How has intercession led you to share the gospel with deeper awareness or bolder practice?

_____

_____

_____

5. *Our gospel fluency comes alive when we proclaim it from this posture of victory in Christ, even as we struggle in our language.* Consider how language learning challenges may be a part of your personal testimony.

_____

_____

_____

My Next Faithful Step

Describe one way you resolve to put what you have learned from Chapter 11 *God Speaks My Language* into practice.

_____

_____

_____

12

Pilgrims

Goal: Identify as a Kingdom pilgrim, with an unwavering assurance in your destination and an insatiable desire to invite others to join you from the "nations of every language" (Zechariah 8:23).

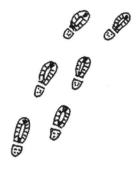

The greater journey is that he pursues us.

I am honored to participate in house church in our new city with a group of young families and singles who week after week share updates on life, language, culture, and gospel ministry. They all came to live in this big city following Jesus' gospel commission. Sometimes I get this mental picture of us all camping, only not in the woods, but in a big, stress-filled, Central Asian city, and it's not just for the weekend, it's for life.

And that's often how I see these precious brothers and sisters. They've made some radical choices to do some crazy things with their lives and families (Luke 9:61-2). I'm reminded of Christian in Bunyan's *Pilgrim's Progress*, "To go back is nothing but death; to go forward is fear of death, and life everlasting beyond it. I will yet go forward."[32]

Everything is new when we come to a place like this. Not shiny-new, either. Difficult-new, rough, hard, bewildering, challenging, tiring, unfamiliar, often unwelcoming-new. Home is far away, and there's a lot about life as we once we knew it, or as we possibly remember it, that feels farther and farther away with each passing day. We can no longer answer the question "Where is home?" I spend a lot of time thinking about these things.

> There's a bit of placelessness in all of us. (Ben, house-church member)

I grew up in a place between worlds. My passport country and where I consider home – two very different places – have never truly reconciled, but that's OK. I've learned to live with the tension of being a *third culture kid* even as an adult. That's probably why I love interacting with other TCKs, especially young people who are in the middle of thinking about what this all means for their lives. I recall one young man recently telling some of his younger TCK friends about his experience returning to his passport country. He described it as just another trip to another country. Final destination – unknown.

The great hope about our life journey as followers of Christ is this: we really *do* have a final destination. Sometimes when we take ourselves out of our familiar sense of home, whether San Francisco or North Carolina, and enter that place of other, whether New York or Istanbul, somehow we jolt awake to the greater journey, that pilgrim-journey that clears our minds and hearts and allows us to see the Kingdom in a new and fresh way.

We are called to proclaim the gospel to our neighbors, at home, or around the world, and this is our gospel pilgrimage. But we need to remember that the greater pilgrimage is about our identity in Christ, that every day God pursues us, and every day he forms us more and more into the image of his son. This is really all the same journey, just seen on two levels. As God transforms our lives with the gospel, every day, everywhere, he calls us to testify of this good news. This is the greater story. This is why we go and proclaim the gospel.

Traveling Light

Take nothing for the road (Luke 9:3).

When I think about traveling light, I think about the Central Asian nomads who traditionally lived in *yurts*, portable, circular, felt-covered tents made from wood, and decorated with embroidered felt rugs. Yurts are held together with camel skin strings and take about an hour to assemble and can be transported by a team of horses or camels.

When I think about the families I church with here in this city, and the constant state of flux so many of us seem to endure in order to sustain life here, it's like we are modern-day nomads in our modern-day yurts. We move to unknown places, living in faith, learning to be nimble as we adjust to life as we now know it, trying to learn some language and culture, and somehow finding spaces where we can begin to thrive in life and ministry. Nothing is easy. We give up a lot.

I think about the disciples who left everything to follow Jesus. I think of Jesus. Jesus personified the ultimate expression of giving up everything for the sake of ultimate love (John 3:16) by leaving heaven and "emptying himself" (Phil 2:7) and coming to be with us. He calls us to do the same. He called fishermen to give up their nets and follow him (Mark 1:18).

In Luke 9, when people said they would follow him, he reminded them "that foxes have dens, and birds of the air have nests, but the Son of Man has no place to lay His head" (v. 58). When one asked to bury his father, he told them to let the dead bury their dead (vv. 59-60). Another wanted to say good-bye but Jesus told him not to look back (vv. 61-62).

Jesus, "who for the joy that lay before him endured the cross, despising the shame" (Hebrews 12:2) calls us to radically give up everything to follow him (Matthew 16:24-28, Mark 8:34 - 9:1, Luke 9:23-27), and he knows exactly what that feels like.

Jesus equips us for ministry in ways that seem counter-intuitive, minimal. Even when it seems impossible, Jesus gives us everything we need, somehow, including the language. But we need to depend on him completely. He equips, he empowers, he commissions, but it often does not feel that way.

In the beginning of Luke 9, Jesus called the twelve together and gave them power and authority (v. 1) and then he sent them to proclaim the gospel, the kingdom of God, and to heal (v. 2). He told them to take nothing for the journey "no staff, no bag, no bread, no money; and don't take an extra shirt" (v. 3). The instructions were specific, the equipment, minimal. The Bible says they preached the gospel and healed everywhere (v. 6).

Immediately after the apostles returned and told Jesus everything they had done, they withdrew to Bethsaida, presumably to be alone (v. 10). However, the crowds learned of this and followed them. Jesus spent the entire day teaching the people and ministering to them. The day wore on, so the twelve came to Jesus and told him to send the crowd away to find lodging and provisions in the nearby villages and countryside, for they were in a desolate place (v. 12). But Jesus said to them, "You give them something to eat" (v. 13).

Isn't that interesting? Jesus had just taken the disciples through an amazing lesson in complete and total dependence on the power and provision of God when he had commissioned them to preach the kingdom of God and heal throughout the villages. Immediately upon returning and reporting to Jesus everything that God had done through them, they once again were faced with the dilemma of trying to figure out how to respond to Jesus' command in obedience and faith.

The best they could come up with was, "We have no more than five loaves and two fish – unless we are to go and buy food for all these people" (v. 14). That's probably the best I could have come up with. Jesus then tells the disciples to feed 5000 men, plus women and children, with this handful of loaves and fishes. In the same way, Jesus puts us in situations where we must depend on him completely. Communicating the gospel in another language can sometimes feel this way. And it sometimes feels just as risky. We're asked to give up a lot, enter into high-risk situations, and do things we could never, ever do on our own.

What have we got to lose?

The farther you go with God, the more you have to give up.[33]

The pilgrim identity comes to us on several levels. When we journey into new cultures and languages, our identities completely shift. Everything we are experiencing is new on the outside, and it feels like everything is changing on the inside.

God is well aware of these changes, and, in fact, is intimately involved with all that is going on within us, and he uses these changes in our lives – those happening on the outside and on the inside – to reshape us and bring us into alignment with who we are in Christ. He radically forms us into the kingdom people he wants us to be – vibrant, nimble, and ready to bear his glory, and to be his ambassadors among the lost.

God shapes us into his image for his purposes as we enter other cultures and learn other languages. This is perhaps the greatest journey of all for us – the inward and downward journey – as we become kingdom-pilgrims of the gospel.

"Then Peter responded to Him, 'See, we have left everything and followed you. So what will there be for us?'" (Matt 19:27). What actually do we risk losing when we choose to communicate the gospel in another language that we don't know well – but are learning – among people who may view us with suspicion, where we indeed risk being misunderstood on several levels?

We are called to the journey of the Great Commission. Our journey, our pilgrimage, has everything to do with how we host the presence of Christ in and through our lives among our lost neighbors in places where Christ is not known.

And that's what I think keeps the people in my church learning language, sharing Christ, praying for their neighbors, loving their families well, and living this crazy Central Asian nomadic life, in concrete yurts, in the big bustling city, day after day, year after year. Their fervency, their joy – it defies reason.

He is no fool who gives what he cannot keep, to gain what he cannot lose. (Jim Elliot)

We Come from a Long Line of Nomads

I guess we can blame Abraham for starting us out on this nomadic journey of faith. God called Abraham to leave his home, and go to a place he would show him. Abraham obeyed God, and literally lived for the rest of his life in tents, on the move, watching his son's generation, and his grandson's generation grow up around him, living in tents, on the move, wandering through the land that God had promised them, living as foreigners in that land, and holding onto the future promise of inheritance.

By faith Abraham, when he was called, obeyed and set out for a place that he was going to receive as an inheritance. He went out, even though he did not know where he was going. By faith he stayed as a foreigner in the land of promise, living in tents as did Isaac and Jacob, coheirs of the same promise. For he was looking forward to the city that has foundations, whose architect and builder is God (Hebrews 11:8-10).

And that kind of perspective – one that envisions the future promise of God and lives in expectation of its fulfillment, in full-throttle faith – just doesn't make sense until we begin to understand that God's kingdom is our final destination. And this journey to his kingdom may take us to the unfamiliar new language or new culture, compelling us to live with great faith and share the hope we have in Christ with all those whom we encounter on this pilgrim path.

One of the most vibrant images of our kingdom pilgrimage is prophesied by Zechariah about the exiles returning from captivity. This is a word of great hope to those returning to Jerusalem, the city of their ancestors, which they had never seen. But it is also a word of great hope for all of us traveling to the city of God, his dwelling place.

The Lord of Armies says this: "Peoples will yet come, the residents of many cities; the residents of one city will go to another, saying: Let's go at once to plead for the Lord's favor and to seek the Lord of Armies. I am also going. Many peoples and strong nations will come to seek the Lord of Armies in Jerusalem and to plead for the Lord's favor." The Lord of Armies says this: "In those days, ten men from nations of every language will grab the robe of a Jewish man tightly, urging: Let us go with you, for we have heard that God is with you" (Zechariah 8:20-23).

These exiles, these pilgrims, were on a journey of hope, of vision, and of invitation. Their hope was in a promise to return to the city of God, the same city Abraham hoped for, whose architect and builder is God. Their vision was a city filled with the peace and very presence of God. We catch a glimpse into this vision, a city filled with laughter, joy, and deep contentment.

> The Lord of Armies says this: "Old men and women will again sit along the streets of Jerusalem, each with a staff in hand because of advanced age. The streets of the city will be filled with boys and girls playing in them" (Zechariah 8:4-5).

This was their invitation, as it is ours. There is something magnetically compelling about this whole scene which our souls long for – the palpable peace of God, his dwelling place, his Kingdom. We each have inklings of Eden. We yearn to be invited.

Consider the immensity of this prophetic word – not just for the exiles returning to the land of their fathers, but also for us, as we envision a journey toward our destination during which ten men from the nations of every language grab our robe, shirt, or jacket, and beg us to take them with us (8:23). Can we put ourselves into this kingdom dynamic? Isn't this what drives us to the nations, to live as neighbors among them, and to share the gospel with them? It is this vision that motivates us to plant our lives into a 21st Century Great Commission location among neighbors whose languages we learn so we can share with them the good news of the Kingdom. Our God reigns. Our God saves.

Identity Shift

Our motivation is the Lord Himself. He must be our joy, our passion, our satisfaction, and ultimate fulfillment. His complete forgiveness and acceptance of us must be the foundation of all we do. No 'high vocation' or spiritual achievements in life can ever fill that vacuum in our hearts.[34]

Thinking back, when I consider the precious people in my church, what is really happening to us when we actually move to new places, enter other cultures, and learn different languages? Research indicates that we certainly change when we do this. Our identities necessarily change as we adapt to other cultures and learn new languages. This is a normal part of the interpersonal cross-cultural engagement process. It's also a major contributor to the stress we endure as we encounter and invest in new cultures and languages. In our city, often even answering the simplest questions in our new language – questions about who we are and what we do – can be surprisingly disorienting. We find ourselves having to manage a growing sense of uprootedness, placelessness and restlessness as we try to orient our lives within this completely new culture and language. We do our best to create simple truthful responses to the most basic questions like these, though they tend to roll around in our minds and hearts as we continue to ask ourselves: "Who are we here and now, in this place? And just what have we gotten ourselves into?"

So, the real question is not whether we change, rather how we manage to invest in this change when we are faced with the challenges of learning another language and entering a new culture. This represents a huge shift in the way others may view us and the way we view ourselves as our personal life settings become increasingly complex: how we communicate, how we see the world, how we respond to others who see the world differently from us, and so on.

Ultimately, entering into a new language and cultural setting represents a fundamental shift in our identity. The more we engage and immerse, and the more language we learn, the more we change.

We really cannot stop this process, and there's a danger in trying. We can hide out in same-culture enclaves, isolating ourselves from the people around us. Or we can drown ourselves in work, meetings, or travel. Whatever the reason or excuse, our lives can quickly reduce to a shadow of who we are called to be if we stop growing in the language of our neighbor. Only when our second language identity ossifies does our language cease to grow.

Some of the most compelling and inspiring research into the dynamic of second language identity introduces the concept of a *second-language vision*, or envisioning the personal changes we anticipate as we learn a new language. Essential to any new language task, we need to envision our *second-language-selves*, and what it may take for us to move toward this vision.

How do we see ourselves right now in our native language? How do we see ourselves in our second language – perhaps at present? In the future? Are our *second-language-future-self* visions plausible? Are they within reach? Are we afraid about anything related to who we see ourselves becoming in our new language? Perhaps we have a fear of failing, or a fear of the unknown, or just a fear of our new language? Are we in touch with our here-and-now selves enough to know how they affect our *future selves*, or our visions for the future?

Zoltán Dörnyei has done what frankly I consider to be breathtaking research on this subject of second language (L2) motivation, conclusively testifying to a superior identity for those motivated by a vision preceding even a second-language vision; that is, a divine vision, and a divine text driving that vision.

> We have found that when the three key components examined in this study – divine call/vision, L2 learning vision, and a sacred text – are pooled, synchronized, and channeled meaningfully, they appear to generate

an unusually high "jet stream" of motivation for language learning. Learners are caught in a powerful inner current that propels them to acquire language with exceptional intensity, persistence, and longevity.[35]

Pause to consider what this actually means for our identities as we enter new languages and cultures. As followers of Christ and as people of the gospel, we indeed have a sacred vision, a sacred text, and a holy and great commission which defines our call and shapes who we are to the very core. When Jesus commissioned us to take the gospel to all peoples, he promised to empower us and to be with us. This means that as we are called, we are empowered to teach the gospel to all nations. By faith, our effort is to learn the language, and adapt to the culture, for the sake of the gospel. But it is this very effort, fueled by our sacred vision and calling, that draws us into this jet-stream of learning, defined by a deep, Spirit-filled, abiding motivation to live and share the gospel with every breath we take.

As Jesus calls us, he empowers us to live the impossible task of taking the gospel to the "nations of every language" (Zechariah 8:23). Indeed, we may find our personal identities shaken to the core. We may struggle to muster courage and resilience to press on. We may even come to the brink of giving up. I know I have. I'm pretty sure many from my church have. I'm pretty sure we all have.

Humility

The downward journey is a gospel story.[36]

So, what gives us the courage and tenacity to press on and learn language well as we take on a second language identity? Core to our identity is our relationship with Christ. And yet, in the process of learning a language and going across cultures, there is a certain attitude that necessarily accompanies our identity in Christ that allows this shift, this incarnation, to happen with grace.

This attitude is found in one word: humility. There is a strong connection between humility and the transformation of our identities. When we are called to teach the gospel to all peoples, we are called to an intentional shift in our identities, a process requiring humility and patience, as well as courage and endurance.

What we need to remember is that our identity shift is already happening in our spirits (2 Corinthians 5:17), and therefore we must press in to believe that God is shaping us into who we are in him, to display the gospel in word and deed, in signs and wonders, to our lost neighbors. People will see and know the salvation of God when they see it displayed in our lives.

So, our identity in our new culture is a display of the attitude that was in Christ Jesus (Philippians 2:5-8). And this is simply confirmation that God is already transforming our lives, and we are therefore on display for the lost to see and hear the gospel (2 Corinthians 2:14). Andrew Murray says it best:

> Believer! Study the humility of Jesus. This is the secret, the hidden root of your redemption. Sink down into it deeper day by day. Believe with your whole heart that this Christ, whom God has given you, even as His divine humility wrought the work for you, will enter in to dwell and work within you too, and make you what the Father would have you be.[37]

God takes us on the same downward journey that he took his son. The incarnation of Jesus is our supreme example of humility. Paul invited the Philippian church to join Jesus on this journey. God invites us on this journey also.

We must take on the posture of humility, compassion, and love, as well as a willingness to suffer personal loss for the glory of Christ among the unreached. This includes an enthusiasm to embrace the challenge of a new language and a new language-related self, to "become all things to all people" (1 Corinthians 9:22) as we consider the gospel for the unreached in "regions beyond" (2 Corinthians 10:16).

Our lost neighbors will vividly see the gospel in our witness; our verbal witness to the gospel of Christ, as well as the testimony of the redemptive work of God in our lives, as we enter into their lives and learn to communicate the gospel to them with understanding. This is a walk of faith that we experience, and that they will see.

Paul – 2 Corinthians

One of the most compelling life stories of the gospel across cultures is found in the testimony of the apostle Paul. God called Paul to take the gospel to the Gentiles (Ephesians 3:1-8, Acts 9:15, Acts 22:21, Romans 1:14), to "regions beyond" (2 Corinthians 10:16), "where Christ had not been named" (Romans 15:18-20). Paul understood this to include people who were completely unknown to him, wholly unreached, "excluded from the citizenship of Israel, and foreigners to the covenants of the promise, without hope and without God in the world" (Ephesians 2:12).

Paul "became all things to all people", in order that some might be saved (1 Corinthians 9:22). In other words, the further and deeper Paul ventured into the world of his Gentile neighbors to preach and display the gospel of Jesus Christ, the more God formed Paul into the image of his Son, to be his witness.

Paul departed from all he had known as a Jew and entered into the world of the Gentiles – barbaric, polytheistic, animistic, atheistic, unwelcoming, dangerous, unfriendly. In many ways, he was signing his own death warrant. Live or die, he was never the same person again.

Arguably the most personal and autobiographical of his letters, 2 Corinthians vividly captures Paul's life among the Gentiles transformed by the power of the gospel. Paul opens his heart to this church through this letter in ways that allow us in a sense to join him on the journey, to see how he actually lived the gospel he preached. Maybe we're in a small house in Achaia with a group of believers listening as the apostle shares from his life over lamplight. Or perhaps we're walking the lonely Roman road bound for the next Asian village, listening to Paul talk about the gospel. We are taken down paths of painful risk, radical joy, deep humility, and profound boldness as Paul gives his life away for the gospel among all peoples.

"We don't want you to be unaware, brothers and sisters, of our affliction that took place in Asia" (2 Corinthians 1:8). I don't think we can overstate the intensity of Paul's life, in the sense that he and his companions felt completely overwhelmed, beyond strength, despairing even of life. Near death, they put their hope in God, and God delivered them; God, who raises the dead. And they trusted that God would rescue them again (1:8-10). They fully expected to face death, and fully put their hope in God. This was just life as they knew it. It doesn't get any more real than this.

Persecuted by his own people, Paul gave up a lot to take the gospel to the Gentiles. Rejected and ridiculed, Paul worked with all of his energy to make the message of the gospel clear and accessible to those who were wholly unlike him. He willingly departed from his identity as a prominent Jew, soberly aware of the suffering and rejection he would endure for the sake of God's glory among the Gentiles. This is how he chose to live. This is how he counted the cost.

Through all of this it was God – the "God of all comfort" – who comforted Paul and his companions in their affliction, so that they would be able to comfort those who were experiencing affliction, with the comfort with which they themselves were comforted by God (1:3-4). Paul knew affliction, and he knew the supernatural abiding comfort of God. Paul knew weakness and peril, and he intimately knew the daily deliverance and salvation of God (1:5-6).

Paul gave about as much attention to his suffering in this letter as he did to the deliverance and salvation he found in Christ. These two dynamics were inseparable in his mind. Core to his identity, Paul's affliction was a distinct and sure pathway to God's glory through the entire span of his life and ministry, which Paul described throughout the letter (7:5-7; 6:4-10; 11:21-33). Paul's testimony was one of both suffering and victory; one did not come without the other. Paul's identity in Christ was completely consumed by the gospel – displaying it and proclaiming it. Paul gave up everything for the sake of the gospel, and in return he gained everything for the sake of Christ.

Paul identifies less as a Jew, and more as simply a follower of Christ. Finding common ground where he not only could honestly identify with his Gentile neighbors, he was able to bring them great hope.

Though Paul was clearly seen as a foreigner in places of ministry among the Gentiles, he most supremely identified himself as a follower of Christ (2:14). Everything about Paul's life – his words, his deeds, his very identity – was consumed by the gospel and the glory of Christ through all of life's experiences, the aroma of life to those being saved, and the aroma of death to those who were perishing (2:15). Paul entered situations and engaged people with the gospel, fully aware that he hosted the very presence of Christ in his life, representing the integrity and sincerity of his ministry, and that is what made all the difference.

"Who is adequate for these things? For we do not market the word of God for profit like so many. On the contrary, we speak with sincerity in Christ, as from God and before God" (2:16-17). This mindset set the course for Paul's life and became the over-arching theme of all he taught throughout this letter.

Everything came back to the presence and power of God in his life. It was God who was at work in his life, and in the lives of all whom he encountered. Paul's singular persuasion was borne of the miraculous transforming power of gospel. He was called to live it and proclaim it.

The gospel characterized Paul's life, witness, and work. By their own lives these Corinthian believers represented the fruit of Paul's loving labor among them, written on his heart. They testified to Paul's faithfulness because of their transformed hearts and lives, "not written with ink but with the Spirit of the living God – not on tablets of stone but on tablets of human hearts" (3:3).

Along with Paul, we marvel and celebrate the mystery of the gospel. Paul nailed it by comparing what we experience when we come to the Lord, with this highwater mark of the revelation of God's glory in the Old Testament. Though we can hardly fathom the glory Moses experienced on the mountain, and the glory of God in his face, how much more mysterious and awesome is the glory that rests upon us as believers in Christ! (3:7-18). "We all, with unveiled faces, are looking as in a mirror at the glory of the Lord and are being transformed into the same image from glory to glory; this is from the Lord who is the Spirit" (3:18).

As we experience God's glory in such a powerful, generative, and direct way, it puts things in right perspective. God has made us competent to be ministers of a new covenant, not of the letter, but of the Spirit (3:6, 17). Who indeed is sufficient for such a ministry (3:5)? There is nothing that we can do in our own capacity to effect the heart-transformation that so mysteriously and gloriously grips the lives of people who inherit salvation. This is the supernatural work of God in each soul.

Paul's ministry bore witness to the splendor of the gospel in his life. A veil may cover the hearts and minds of many. The god of this age may blind them. There may be overwhelming darkness. But Paul encourages us not to lose heart. "For God who said, 'Let light shine out of darkness,' has shone in our hearts to give the light of the knowledge of God's glory in the face of Jesus Christ" (4:6).

Paul described the gospel as this extraordinary power contained in "jars of clay," the salvation of God on display in his life (4:7), so that people would know this gospel came from God. Can we not identify with this? Isn't this good news, that the severity of our unworthiness is actually what God selects to house and display the splendor of the gospel, through our lives for all to see? This, too, is our testimony, our proclamation, that only by God's marvelous grace are we saved.

In so many ways we can agree with Paul, "We are afflicted in every way, but not crushed; perplexed, but not driven to despair; persecuted, but not forsaken; struck down, but not destroyed (4:8-9). We carry in our body the death of Jesus" (4:10). The life-giving power of the gospel on display through our affliction – as our mortal flesh is given over to death – displays the life of Jesus in our lives and in the lives of those who receive the gospel from our witness. "For we who live are always being given over to death for Jesus's sake, so that Jesus's life may also be displayed in our mortal flesh. So then, death is at work in us, but life in you" (4:11-12).

Our fluency in the gospel among our lost neighbors, in the end, is really less about our persuasive eloquence and more about the vibrant and living testimony of the gospel on display in our lives. We believe in the simple familiar stories of the gospel because they represent changed lives, including our lives! It is a privilege to daily live out our faith before our lost neighbors so that they can witness the gospel at work in us, a tangible testimony to them. A coworker recently wrote,

> This week I met with Alev for coffee. I was able to share my testimony, after being interrupted several times, and talked about sacrifices and how Jesus is our

ultimate sacrifice. I shared John 3:16-17 with her and told her that Jesus died for our sins. She quickly stopped me and said, "No, he died for your sins, but he didn't die for my sins."

One of the brothers in my church recently shared this response he received from his secular educated neighbor, "I can accept that God is love, but I cannot accept what they did to Jesus on the cross."

Comments and perspectives like these are common in our part of the world. When we confront our lost neighbors with the gospel, and appeal to them to be reconciled to Christ, they may be confounded, perhaps offended, or simply uninterested. What do we do with this? Do we give up, lose heart? No, we press on (4:1,16). We continue telling our lost neighbors the good news of Jesus. We continue entreating them to be reconciled to God.

Until our neighbors are drawn by God, through spiritual conviction, to come to the foot of the cross in repentance for their sins, they cannot understand the meaning of Jesus' sacrifice. Until their hearts turn from prideful offense toward abject poverty of soul, from indifference to sin, to godly grief (7:10-11) leading to overflowing thankfulness that God would look upon their unworthy state and save them, they cannot enter the Kingdom of Heaven.

Therefore, we persist in our appeal. God loves our neighbors. God loves Alev. I am thankful Alev heard the gospel and I pray she hears it again and repents. "He made the one who did not know sin to be sin for us, so that in him we might become the righteousness of God" (5: 21).

No other purpose compelled Paul to risk his life and suffer for the gospel among Gentiles throughout the Roman world than the love of Christ (5:14). God saved him, and changed him, completely. Paul staked his life on the life-giving power of the gospel (5:17). Paul's task was singular – to represent Christ. His appeal, simple – be reconciled to God (5:19-20).

"See, now is the acceptable time; now is the day of salvation!" (6:2).

Paul presents himself to the Corinthians in a sincere effort to not be a stumbling block to anyone. He and his companions "commend themselves" (6:4), "opening their hearts" (6:11) with a deeply personal appeal, a whole-hearted testimony to how they have lived, witnessing to what they know to be true, displaying the transparent gospel with their very lives. It doesn't get any more personal than this:

> By great endurance, by afflictions, by hardships, by difficulties, by beatings, by imprisonments, by riots, by labors, by sleepless nights, by times of hunger, by purity, by knowledge, by patience, by kindness, by the Holy Spirit, by sincere love, by the word of truth, by the power of God; through weapons of righteousness for the right hand and the left, through glory and dishonor, through slander and good report; regarded as deceivers, yet true; as unknown, yet recognized; as dying, yet see – we live; as being disciplined, yet not killed; as grieving, yet always rejoicing; as poor, yet enriching many; as having nothing, yet possessing everything (6:4-10).

Paul's open-hearted testimony is like a 360-degree view of the gospel – vibrant, pungently fragrant, obvious, and beautiful. It's the triumphal procession in Christ (2:14), Christ's aroma (2:15-16), the transformation from one degree of glory to another (3:18), the new creation (5:17). This is the gospel in Paul's life, at every turn, every angle, through all of his life's circumstances. Paul holds nothing back, he lays his life bare, and he testifies to the goodness of God. "We have spoken openly to you, Corinthians; our heart has been opened wide" (6:11).

Paul knows their hearts. He knows they are constrained by their own affections (6:12). He knows they need to give their hearts to the Lord. He speaks to them as his children, "widen your hearts also," with gentle and heart-felt appeal (6:13). Just as he had opened his heart them, he asks the Corinthians to do the same with him, to believe the gospel, to open their hearts to the Lord. Paul lived as one who reconciled people to God through the proclamation of the gospel alive in his heart.

This was the trajectory of Paul's life and ministry. In all areas of life, through all experience, he displayed the gospel, the personal life-changing, normal-defying, power of God in and through his life – a precious gift to the Corinthian church.

In the same way, our lost neighbors need to hear the gospel. They also need to see it lived out, through our lives and testimonies, as we invite them to God, through the heart-wrenching, life-giving power of the gospel found only in Jesus, the author of our salvation. Our investment as cross-cultural ministers of the gospel most essentially is not in the outcomes, results, or completed strategies; rather, it is in the radical, life-changing, impossible-in-our-own-strength obedience to the simple and profound command: Go and make disciples of all peoples.

> Our investment as cross-cultural ministers of the gospel most essentially is not in the outcomes, results, or completed strategies; rather, it is in the radical, life-changing, impossible in-our-own-strength obedience to the simple and profound command: Go and make disciples of all peoples.

When I first met Sean and Kelly, I learned that they were already fluent in another language, had willingly left a thriving ministry in the capable care of national partners, only to begin again from scratch in another part of the world, in a place few believers venture, among an unreached minority people.

The new language they had to learn was tough, with extensive dialectical differences between speakers from different cities, villages, and communities. Often mixed with other languages, just trying to communicate with people in their new language was like nothing they had previously experienced. Sean and Kelly confessed they had to constantly fight off a sense of failure.

We bring nothing to the table.
(Sean and Kelly)

They pressed on faithfully. Every time I saw them, they would talk about visiting in neighbors' homes, drinking tea, and sharing the gospel. They talked about ways they were working on language, learning new stories, and sharing simple testimonies. It was obvious they were desperate to reach gospel fluency out of a deep love for the Lord, and a love for their neighbors. I thought of Paul's loving investment for his Corinthian children, "I will most gladly spend and be spent for you" (12:15).

I soon began hearing about some of these neighbors coming to Christ. Sean and Kelly continued learning, sharing, and pouring their lives into these new believers. As Paul invested his life in the Corinthian believers for the sake of the gospel, this is exactly how I saw Sean and Kelly spending their lives. Borne from a radical faith and hope in God, they lovingly and persistently invested in the lives of their neighbors, learned language, and faithfully ministered the gospel to them.

Fully aware that they came into this completely empty-handed, they personified what it meant to "die to self" and willingly gave themselves away for the sake of the gospel. Gospel fluency therefore is not simply our ability to share the gospel in our new languages; it's really more about our faith, our faithfulness, and our willingness to die to ourselves.

> Gospel fluency therefore is not simply our ability to share the gospel in our new languages; it's really more about our faith, our faithfulness, and our willingness to die to ourselves.

When I think about Sean and Kelly, and so many others whom I've had the honor to know on this pilgrim journey, I think about my own father. Just as Paul said, "I am not seeking what is yours, but you" (12:14), my dad gladly spent his life on me. He trained me, coached me, counseled me, saved up for me, and swam a thousand seas for me. That's love.

Growing up in Southeast Asia, I had the incredible opportunity to closely watch my father pour his life into many other sons in the faith through the years. I think of Isaac, our neighbor, whom my dad discipled. Isaac eventually moved with his bride and infant daughter to live among and bring the gospel to the unreached villagers of northeast Borneo. Dad would often visit Isaac and Rosie. On one visit the tribal leader's wife passed away. She was a believer. At the funeral, Isaac and Dad reminded them that as followers of Christ we have eternal hope. What followed was a time of celebration and astonishment because, as the chief told Isaac and my dad, "We are honored that God has chosen one of us to populate heaven!"

Some of my best memories growing up are hearing Dad tell stories of the gospel like this one. My parents are pilgrims. They spent their lives among the unreached in "regions beyond" (10:16); they learned languages and entrusted the gospel to many sons and daughters; they led people to faith, discipled new believers, counseled young couples, met in homes for prayer and worship, started churches, and did all of this wherever the Lord took them. And they had the joy of watching many of these disciples, just like Isaac and Rosie, take the gospel to regions beyond and disciple others (2 Timothy 2:2).

"Didn't we walk in the same spirit and in the same footsteps?" (2 Corinthians 12:18). Maybe this is what being pilgrims is all about; an unwavering assurance in our destination, and an insatiable desire to invite others – from the "nations of every language" (Zechariah 8:23) – to join us. "How beautiful are the feet of those who bring good news" (Isaiah 52:7, Romans 10:15). Anybody can be a nomad, traveling from place to place. It takes a deeper investment to be a pilgrim, to have ears that hear, eyes that see, and a heart that yields.

Chapter Summary

- Our identity as Kingdom pilgrims.
- Paul's testimony from 2 Corinthians

Reflect and Respond

1. *When we journey into new cultures and languages, our identities completely shift. Everything we are experiencing is new on the outside, and it feels like everything is changing on the inside.* As you reflect on this statement, how do you see yourself in your new language right now? How about a year from now? Be specific. (E.g., I am sitting in a chai house in the evening with a neighbor talking about...)

_____

_____

2. You know the cross-cultural identity shift is coming. Have you ever experienced this kind of personal shift or change before? Share one thing you feel, think, or anticipate, and how you hope to respond.

_____

_____

3. How did these chapters or readings from 2 Corinthians help you to better understand your own identity in Christ and your call to live a gospel-fluent life in your new language and culture?

_____

_____

4. *Paul departed from all he had known as a Jew and entered into the world of the Gentiles; barbaric, polytheistic, animistic, atheistic, unwelcoming, dangerous, unfriendly – in many ways, he was signing his own death warrant. Live or die, he was never the same person again.* Read 1 Corinthians 9:22. What is one adjustment you can make in your life where you can, like Paul, become all thing to all people, so that some of your neighbors might be saved? How would this adjustment effect your life choices?

_____

_____

My Next Faithful Step

Describe one way you resolve to put what you have learned from Chapter 12 *Pilgrims* into practice.

_____

_____

Conclusion

More from 2 Corinthians

Maybe this is what being pilgrims is all about; an unwavering assurance in our destination, and an insatiable desire to invite others-from the "nations of every language" (Zechariah 8:23) - to join us.

We have great hope in Christ, especially as language learners and cross-cultural workers, as we consider our common pursuit to take the gospel to "lands beyond" (2 Corinthians 10:16). Paul brings us back to a strong and purposeful reminder, both to the church, and to us his readers, of his personal and profound insufficiency to pursue such a vision and task (2:16). We are completely and fully dependent on the power of Christ and the gospel as we consider any assignment to which God calls us.

"If boasting is necessary, I will boast about my weaknesses" (11:30). Paul enters into the final stretch of this letter reminding us of the overarching theme of his identity in

Christ: a complete eradication of all personal commendation, with all boasting in the Lord, and all approval from the Lord (12:17-18).

Paul's life in many ways represented a paradox. When confronted with the need to validate his spiritual authority in his defense against false teachers (11:13), he could have boasted about as much. The sheer volume and intensity of meritorious experiences he endured is absolutely mind-blowing (11:23-33). We begin to understand just a little bit more what daily life must have been like for Paul – the intensity, the agony, the stress. Yet Paul did not boast in any of this, considering it all foolish (11:21).

Paul spoke of visions and revelations in the Lord, being caught up into the third heaven, "hearing inexpressible words, which a human being is not allowed to speak" (12:1-4). Again, Paul could have boasted in all of this. Rather, speaking about this experience in third person, Paul concluded, "I will boast about this person, but not about myself, except of my weaknesses" (12:6).

These verses provide us a deeper look at what seems to be core to Paul's pilgrim identity as he willingly entered into a position of weakness, a dynamic humility, reaching the end of himself, and his abilities; he put himself on the altar – his identity, dignity, honor, his sense of accomplishment – and fully trusted in Christ, depending on Christ's strength in all things. This position of weakness was the identity Paul willingly, actively, joyfully embraced. "Paul's own weakness in the work was part of God's design for the work" (David Platt).

We will never be weaker in our gospel proclamation ability than we are now. (Mel, as a word of encouragement to fellow learners.)

And yet there's more. Paul points to something even more significant that happened to him in the wake of all the suffering, visions, and revelations that brought him to an even deeper and more profound awareness of who he really was in Christ: he was given a thorn in the flesh, a messenger of Satan, to afflict him. Paul pleaded with the Lord three times to be released from this suffering (12:7-8). Christ responded to him, grafting this message onto Paul's identity: "My grace is sufficient for you, for my power is perfected in weakness" (12:9) to which Paul concluded, "Therefore, I will most gladly boast all the more about my weaknesses, so that Christ's power may reside in me. So, I take pleasure in weaknesses, insults, hardships, persecutions, and in difficulties, for the sake of Christ. For when I am weak, then I am strong" (12:9-10).

> We have a cultural perception that causes us to believe that dependence and vulnerability are weaknesses. On the contrary, the one who authenticates his life-message is the one whose strength lies in his willingness to be vulnerable. Jesus' willingness to go all the way to the cross is the supreme example of vulnerability being a strength.[38]

Paul rejoiced even more in his complete and utter weakness. He understood that when he was weak, then he was strong. Paul embraced a life of complete faith and dependence on Christ's strength – even through suffering and pain – to bear the testimony of the gospel to the Gentiles. The strength of his testimony was not found in great and powerful revelations, rather in suffering and weakness; more specifically, in Christ's life-changing power and strength in and through personal weakness. This was the capstone of the gospel in Paul's life.

We often need to see things upside-down. (Ben, house-church member)

169

The paradox in all this is that Paul, already afflicted from the many trials of his life, asked repeatedly for this thorn in his flesh to be removed – something God could have so easily done – yet, it remained a source of pain and affliction, faith and humility, reminding Paul all the more of his weakness, of his complete dependence on the mercy and power of Christ. So, Paul's perspective on life and success, crazy as it may seem at times, was not one of disappointment in his personal limitations, rather one of great hope in the power of God to work in and through the suffering and weakness of his life. "So let the one who boasts, boast in the Lord. For it is not the one commending himself who is approved, but the one the Lord commends" (10:17-18).

In light of that, consider Paul's defense of his weakness: God's strength was his strength. We should never consider our language learning pursuit a liability to the gospel. Our struggle may indeed be the very attitude and posture that God is forming in our souls for the ministry to which he has called us. Is it possible that God works his strength through our weakness for the sake of the gospel? We believe this, but when it comes to our basic communicative ability, it sounds strange, doesn't it? It just does not follow that the gospel can be clearly proclaimed when our language is weak. But the bottom line is, our language could always be stronger than it is, right? Is it possible that God actually is able to, and chooses to demonstrate his strength to us, in us, and through us for the sake of the gospel as we endure weak language ability?

I'm still trying to picture this: In what possible way could Paul exhibit strength through weakness? Or let's look at it more personally: how can we live this out when we experience the pain of weakness in our ministry? Any cross-cultural worker would need to honestly admit to the reality of painful and exposing challenges we all face, including learning another language, often accompanied by extended debilitating seasons of struggle, doubt, and weakness, through which we may just find it hard to rejoice in the strength of the Lord. The reality is, we are weak; and yet, we are strong, because our hope is in Christ and in his promises. This paradox is one of the most confusing and yet most liberating promises in all of scripture and is particularly meaningful for us as we pursue gospel fluency across cultures.

Summary

- Our investment as cross-cultural ministers of the gospel most essentially is not in the outcomes, results, or completed strategies; rather, it is in the radical, life-changing, impossible-in-our-own-strength obedience to the simple and profound command: Go and make disciples of all peoples.

- Gospel fluency therefore is not simply our ability to share the gospel in our new languages; it's really more about our faith, our faithfulness, and our willingness to die to ourselves.

Reflect and Respond

1. How do you understand 2 Corinthians 12:9-10 in light of your personal identity in Christ as you pursue a gospel-fluent life in your new language and culture?

_____

_____

_____

2. As you reflect on the two statements (above) describe how your understanding of *gospel fluency across cultures* has been sharpened or changed?

_____

_____

3. How has this perspective shaped how you envision learning a language?

_____

_____

_____

My Next Faithful Step

After reflecting upon and responding to what you've read in this conclusion to the *1000 Cups of Tea: Field Guide*, describe one way you resolve to put what you have learned into practice.

_____

_____

_____

Articles, lessons, and resources related to *1000 Cups of Tea: Field Guide* can be found at www.language180.com or by scanning this QR code using your camera app.

language 180

My Next Steps to Gospel Fluency

Instructions: Look over the "next faithful steps" you wrote after each chapter. Now summarize your thoughts in the box below to represent how you see yourself pursuing *gospel fluency across cultures*.

Endnotes

[1] I first heard this term used by church planters as they equipped co-workers for ministry among unreached people groups throughout Central Asia. See Jeff Vanderstelt's insightful book *Gospel Fluency* (Crossway 2017).

[2] H. and G. Taylor, *Hudson Taylor's Spiritual Secret*, (Moody Press, Chicago, 1987), 192. I received this little book as a gift (and have carted it with me ever since) while listening to Hudson Taylor III appeal to the churches of Singapore to take the gospel into China. It made a lasting impression on me that he preached in Chinese while his Chinese colleague interpreted into English.

[3] Ibid., 135-75.

[4] https://www.desiringgod.org/messages/the-ministry-of-hudson-taylor-as-life-in-christ

[5] Taylor, *Hudson Taylor's Spiritual Secret*, 230.

[6] https://www.desiringgod.org/messages/the-ministry-of-hudson-taylor-as-life-in-christ

[7] Taylor, *Hudson Taylor's Spiritual Secret*, 235.

[8] Elliot Clark, *Evangelism as Exiles: Life on Mission as Strangers in Our Own Land*, (The Gospel Coalition, 2019), 67. From his experience as a church planter in Central Asia, Clark reminds us to live by three convictions in proclaiming the gospel: 1) Be prepared to offend (authority), 2) Call for response (urgency), and 3) Delight in the gospel (worship). He expresses this third conviction in a profoundly personal and compelling way, "We must recognize that the apologetic force of our preaching isn't always that our message is more believable than another, but that it's more desirable. In evangelism, we don't simply make a logical case, but a doxological one. We aren't just talking to brains. We're speaking to hearts that have desires and eyes that look for beauty. We're not merely trying to convince people that our gospel is true, but that our God is good. Over the years I've tried to move away from cold, structured arguments into exultations of praise. From giving evidence of the resurrection, to reveling in its glory. From merely explaining why Jesus is needed, to showing why he should be wanted. From defending the Bible's truthfulness to rejoicing in its sweetness."

[9] https://www.actfl.org

[10] Evil eye: "An impersonal, amoral force responsible for misfortune, applied to objects both animate and inanimate, providing meaning to people's lives in the sense that it creates a cause-and-effect explanation, perhaps even an underlying connectedness between the metaphysical and physical realities of the universe." See also Bruce Privatsky, *Muslim Turkistan: Kazak Religion and Collective Memory*. Surrey: Curzon Press. 2001.

[11] Nik Ripken, *The Insanity of God* (B&H, 2013), 86.

[12] New Hope, https://www.multiplyhealing.org.

[13] Thomas E. Brewster, 1983. *Language Learning and Mission*, A LEARN! Video seminar for YWAM participants, unpublished transcription, Buchloe, Switzerland. 45. Found in Brewster, Dan. 1997. *Only Paralyzed from the Neck Down*. William Carey Library. Pasadena, CA. 131.

[14] L. Davachi and I. Dobbins, *Declarative Memory*, (Current Directions Psychological Sciences 17-2, 2008) 112-118 as cited in Roy V. H. Pollock, Andy Jefferson, Calhoun W. Wick, *The Six Disciplines of Breakthrough Learning: How to Turn Training and Development into Business Results*, EPUB-ebook (Pfeiffer; 3rd edition, 2015), 122-124.

[15] D. Sousa, *How the Brain Learns* (Corwin, 2011) 134 as cited in Pollock, Jefferson, Wick, *The Six Disciplines of Breakthrough Learning*, 127.

[16] Thor Sawin, Personal notes during our survey trip with teams engaging Central Asians in three urban diaspora contexts, October 2018.

[17] Ibid.

[18] Ibid.

[19] Ibid.

[20] Ibid.

[21] Ibid.

[22] Brewster, 1983. 45. Found in Brewster. 1997. 97-8.

[23] Sawin, 2018.

[24] Ibid.

[25] Ibid.

[26] Ibid.

[27] Joshua Foer, *Moonwalking with Einstein: The Art and Science of Remembering Everything* (New York: Penguin Press, 2011).

[28] Brewster, 1983. 31-2. Found in Brewster. 1997. 270-1.

[29] Ibid., 271.

[30] Clark, *Evangelism as Exiles*, 51.

[31] Zedeke Zemduken, Personal Letter to Author. YWAM. Nicosia, Cyprus, October 23. Found in Brewster. 1997. 269.

[32] John Bunyan, *Pilgrim's Progress* (first published 1678).

[33] Les and Jeannette Maxwell shared this thought over tea one day as we were praying together about their recent trip to visit us in Central Asia.

[34] David Frazier, *Mission Smart,* (Create Space, 2013), 16.

[35] Elfrieda Lepp-Kaethler and Zoltán Dörnyei, "The Role of Sacred Texts in Enhancing Motivation and Living the Vision in Second Language Acquisition", chapter 11 of *Christian Faith and English Language Teaching and Learning* (Mary Shepard Wong, Carolyn Kristjansson, Zoltan Dornyei, ed., Routledge, NY, 2013).

[36] Paul Miller, *A Praying Life* (NavPress, 2017).

[37] Andrew Murray, *Humility,* (first published March 9th, 1895).

[38] T. and E. Brewster, *On Listening to Christ.* 1984. Unpublished Notes. Found in Brewster, 1997. 128.

Made in United States
Orlando, FL
02 March 2022

15290368R00114